Websites

Development

ASP.NET

MVC

Web API

Razor Pages

If you have any questions, comments, or feedback about this book, I would love to hear from you.

Please feel free to reach out to me via email:

Email: ec.books.contact@gmail.com

Table of Contents

Info

The code in this guide was tested on C# 12, .NET 8, and Visual Studio 2022.

There may be certain syntax, code constructs, or concepts that are not explained in some topics, but they will be discussed later to avoid confusing the reader.

This book is written in a minimalistic style and follows a logical flow of topics, allowing you to write programs quickly without unnecessary delays.

Prerequisites

C# - Proficiency in the C# programming language is a must, look for the book Eldar CSharp C# by Eldar Cohen at amazon.

https://www.amazon.com/dp/B0CK3253SR

Basic HTML is mandatory, look for the book HTML by Eldar Cohen at amazon.
https://www.amazon.com/dp/B0CNQG1HD6

CSS - Preferred, but it's not mandatory.

JavaScript - Preferred, but it's not mandatory, look for the book JavaScript by Eldar Cohen at amazon. https://www.amazon.com/dp/B0CQD3SHY4

ASP.NET Introduction

ASP.NET, which stands for Active Server Pages .NET, is a web application framework developed by Microsoft. It provides a wide range of tools and libraries for building web applications, services, and dynamic web content. ASP.NET encompasses several sub-frameworks, including MVC, Razor Pages, Web API, and Blazor, each designed for different aspects of web development.

Frameworks

MVC (Model-View-Controller):

ASP.NET MVC, or simply MVC, is a framework within ASP.NET that adheres to the Model-View-Controller architectural pattern. It helps in structuring web applications by separating them into three key components.

Razor Pages:

Razor Pages is another web application framework within ASP.NET. Unlike MVC, it's more page-centric and doesn't rely on a separate controller. With Razor Pages, the logic is encapsulated in a single Razor Page file. This can be a more straightforward approach for building small to medium-sized applications or for quickly creating web pages.

Web API:

ASP.NET Web API is a framework for building HTTP services that are primarily intended for exposing data and services over HTTP. It's ideal for creating RESTful APIs and is commonly used for building back-end services that are consumed by various clients.

Blazor:

Blazor is a web framework that allows developers to build interactive web applications using C# and .NET, eliminating the need for JavaScript in some scenarios.

Even though there are different frameworks, there are a lot of common things between them.

Development Environment

To develop C# applications, you'll need a code development environment, also called as Integrated Development Environment (IDE)

Popular C# development environments:

1. Visual Studio - the official IDE for C# development by Microsoft

2. Visual Studio Code (VS Code) - lightweight, free, and open-source code editor developed by Microsoft

https://visualstudio.microsoft.com/downloads

Useful Links

ASP.NET apps documentation: https://learn.microsoft.com/en-us/aspnet/core

HTTP status codes: https://learn.microsoft.com/en-us/troubleshoot/developer/webapps/iis/www-administration-management/http-status-code

Web Page

A web page is a document that is designed to be viewed on the World Wide Web, through a web browser like chrome. Web pages are the building blocks of websites and are created using various technologies, including HTML, CSS and JavaScript.

HTML

HTML, which stands for Hypertext Markup Language, is the standard language used to create and structure web pages. HTML uses a markup system to define the structure and content of a web page.

HTML is made up of various tags (or elements), each serving a specific purpose. Tags are enclosed in angle brackets, such as <tagname>. Examples include <html>, <head>, <body>, <p>, <a>, and many more.

Create an empty file named 'page.html' with the .html extension, and then add the following HTML template to it:

```
<!DOCTYPE html>
<html>
<head>
  <meta charset="utf-8" />
  <title></title>
</head>
<body>

</body>
</html>
```

<!DOCTYPE html> - Defines the document type and version of HTML. In this case, it specifies that this is an HTML document.

<html> - Root element that wraps the entire HTML document. All other elements are contained within the <html> element.

<head> - Used for including metadata and other non-visible elements of the document, such as character encoding, links to external stylesheets, and the document title.

<meta charset="utf-8" /> - Specifies the character encoding used for the document, which is typically UTF-8. UTF-8 is a character encoding that supports a wide range of characters from different languages.

<title></title> - Define the title of the web page. The text you want to appear in the browser's title bar should be placed between the opening and closing <title> tags.

<body> - This is where the visible content of the web page is defined. You can include text, images, links, forms, and other elements within the <body> section.

Add inside the body tag the elements below and save and open the file page.html with chrome:

```
<h1>Hello world</h1>
<h2>Hello world</h2>
<p>Hello world</p>
```

Hello world

Hello world

Hello world

<h1> - Represents a top-level heading. It's typically used for the main title or heading of a section.

<h2> - Represents a second-level heading. It's used for subsection headings.

<p> - Represents a paragraph of text.

Look here for more html elements:

https://www.w3schools.com/html/default.asp

CSS

CSS, which stands for Cascading Style Sheets, is a stylesheet language used for describing the presentation and formatting of web documents written in HTML, including layout, colors, fonts, and spacing. It allows you to separate the structure and content of a web page (defined in HTML) from its visual appearance.

Add this code inside the head tag:

```
<style>
  h1 {
    color: red;
  }


  h2 {
    color: green;
  }


  p {
    color: blue;
  }
</style>
```

Hello world

Hello world

Hello world

The **<style>** element is used to enclose the CSS code, and it's typically placed in the <head> section of an HTML document.

h1, **h2**, and **p** are selectors that target specific HTML elements:

h1 selects all level 1 headings.

h2 selects all level 2 headings.

p selects all paragraphs.

The color property is used to set the text color for each selected element.

Class

In CSS, a class is a way to select and apply styles to specific HTML elements.

Update the page.html file with the code below:

```
<style>
  h1 {
    color: red;
  }

  h2 {
    color: green;
  }

  .custom-style {
    color: blue;
    font-weight: bold;
    direction: rtl;
  }
</style>

<h1>Hello world</h1>
<h2 class="custom-style">Hello world</h2>
<p class="custom-style">Hello world</p>
```

Hello world

Hello world

Hello world

The **.custom-style** selector defines a class that sets the text color to blue, makes the text bold (increases font weight), and changes the text direction to right-to-left (RTL).

Use the <link> tag to reference an external CSS stylesheet file named "site.css" for separating the styling from the HTML document.

```html
<link rel="stylesheet" href="./site.css" />
```

JavaScript

JavaScript is a client-side programming language that runs in the browser, used for building interactive and dynamic web pages.

Update the page.html file with the code below:

```html
<h1 id="myH1">Hello world</h1>


<script>
    var heading = document.getElementById("myH1");
    heading.style.color = "red";
</script>
```

Hello world

The **<script>** element is placed at the end of the **<body>** section to ensure that the JavaScript code is executed after the HTML element is defined.

The **<script>** tag is an HTML element used to embed or reference external JavaScript code in an HTML document.

With this code, the text color of the **<h1>** element with the id "myH1" will be changed to red when the page is loaded.

document - DOM(Document Object Model), is a programming interface for web documents. It represents the structure of an HTML document in a tree-like form, where each element in the document is a node in the tree. The DOM provides a way for programs and scripts to access and manipulate the content and structure of web documents.

Use the **<script>** tag to reference an external JavaScript file named "site.js" for separating JavaScript code from the HTML document for better code organization and maintainability.

```html
<script src="./site.js"></script>
```

Razor Pages

I've chosen to begin with the Razor Pages framework due to its simplicity, making it easier to grasp. After gaining basic understanding in Razor Pages, I plan to explore the broader range of ASP.NET capabilities on MVC.

Create new project

ASP.NET Core Web App

A project template for creating an ASP.NET Core application with example ASP.NET Core Razor Pages content

| C# | Linux | macOS | Windows | Cloud | Service | Web |

Choose latest .NET framework:

ASP.NET Core Web App   C#

Framework ⓘ

.NET 7.0 (Standard Term Support)

Expected Solution:

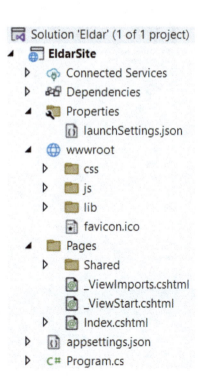

I deleted some stuff from the project to simplify things.

Let's run the project with ctrl + F5

You default browser should pop up and the page Index.cshtml should appear

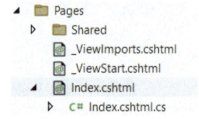

Razor Page consists of two files:

1. Razor Page File(.cshtml) - This file contains the HTML markup along with embedded C# code using the Razor syntax.

2. Page Model File(.cshtml.cs) - This is the code-behind file for the Razor Page. It contains the C# code that complements the .cshtml file. The Page Model file is where you define the page's logic, handle user input, and interact with the data.

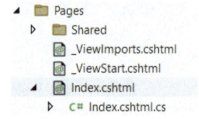

Show data and send data

Update the files below with the code:

Index.cshtml.cs

```csharp
using Microsoft.AspNetCore.Mvc.RazorPages;

namespace EldarSite.Pages
{
    public class IndexModel : PageModel
    {
        public Dictionary<byte,string> Countries = new();

        public void OnGet()
        {
            Countries.Add(1, "Israel");
            Countries.Add(2, "United States");
            Countries.Add(3, "United Kingdom");
        }

        public void OnPost(byte countryCode)
        {
        }
    }
}
```

IndexModel class inherits from **PageModel**. This class is used for handling requests and interactions with a Razor Page.

Countries Dictionary store a collection of countries, with byte values as keys and country names as values.

OnGet Method - Initializing the Countries dictionary, this is done when the page is initially loaded via a GET request.

OnPost Method - Takes a byte parameter countryCode. This method will be called when the page is submitted via a POST request.

Index.cshtml

```
@page "/page"
@model IndexModel

<form method="post">
  <select name="countryCode">
    @foreach (var country in Model.Countries)
    {
      <option value="@country.Key">
        @country.Value
      </option>
    }
  </select>
  <input type="submit" value="send" />
</form>
```

@page - The directive is used to specify the routing url path for the current page.

@model - The directive is used to specify the data associated with the page.

<form> - HTML element is used to collect and submit data from the user to a server. It utilizes the "post" method to send data to the server when the user clicks the "send" button. Typically, the <form> element includes input fields, buttons, and other elements that enable users to enter data.

<select> - HTML dropdown element that allows the user to choose a country, the options for the dropdown are generated dynamically using a foreach loop that iterates through the Model.Countries dictionary defined in the IndexModel class.

<option> - HTML element within the <select> element, representing each key-value pair. The content between the <option> tags is displayed in the browser, while the value attribute remains hidden.

<input> - Input element with type="submit" and value="send", allowing the user to submit their selection.

The form will send a POST request to the server when the user selects a country and clicks the "send" button. The OnPost method in the IndexModel class will be invoked to handle this request.

Run the code:

localhost:7172/page

HTML rendered in the browser:

```html
<form method="post">
  <select name="CountryCode">
    <option value="1">
      Israel
    </option>
    <option value="2">
      United States
    </option>
    <option value="3">
      United Kingdom
    </option>
  </select>
  <input type="submit" value="send" />
</form>
```

Debug the code and click the send button:

```
0 references
public void OnPost(byte countryCode)
{

}
```

countryCode	3

Let's see more ways to pass values

BindProperty

The BindProperty attribute is used to bind properties in your Razor Page model to values sent in HTTP requests. When an HTTP request is made to your Razor Page, if a form field or query parameter has the same name as the property, the data is bound to that property.

```csharp
[BindProperty]
0 references
public byte CountryCode { get; set; }
0 references        CountryCode    1
public void OnPost()
{

}
```

Request

The Request object represents the current HTTP request. It provides access to various aspects of the incoming request, such as the HTTP headers, URL parameters, form data, cookies, and more.

Request.Form is a way to access data submitted from an HTML form using the POST method.

```csharp
public void OnPost()
{
    byte countryCode = byte.Parse(Request.Form["CountryCode"]);
        countryCode    1
}
```

RedirectToPage

After the OnPost method the Index page return without any data, so now we should decide what to do, we can fill the countries list again or we can redirect back to the OnGet method.

```
public IActionResult OnPost()
{
    return RedirectToPage();// Redirect to the OnGet method
}
```

The **RedirectToPage** method is used to perform a server-side redirection to a different Razor Page.

The **IActionResult** interface is used to represent the result of an action method and encapsulate the response that will be sent to the client.

You can redirect to a different internal page by specifying the page path:

```
return RedirectToPage("/Contact");
```

You can redirect to external page with Redirect function:

```
return Redirect("https://www.google.co.il");
```

Program.cs

The Program.cs file serves as the entry point for the application and is used to configure and build the web host.

```
// Creates a new WebApplication builder.
var builder = WebApplication.CreateBuilder(args);

// Adds Razor Pages to the application's services.
builder.Services.AddRazorPages();

//Builds the web application using the builder configuration.
var app = builder.Build();

//This middleware is used to redirect HTTP requests to HTTPS.
app.UseHttpsRedirection();

//This middleware serves static files like HTML, CSS, and
//JavaScript from the application's wwwroot folder.
app.UseStaticFiles();

//This middleware sets up routing for the application.
//It's where you configure URL routing and endpoints.
app.UseRouting();

//Maps Razor Pages, which are typically located in the "Pages"
//folder. It sets up routing for Razor Pages.
app.MapRazorPages();

//Starts the application and listens for incoming requests.
app.Run();
```

Registering services means informing the dependency injection container about the services your application will use.

```
builder.Services.AddRazorPages();
```

Registers services related to Razor Pages in the dependency injection container. This includes services necessary for handling Razor Pages,

Adding components to the request processing pipeline.

19

```
app.MapRazorPages();
```

Configures the request pipeline to handle Razor Pages. It maps a URL path to the Razor Pages middleware, allowing requests to be processed by the Razor Pages engine.

Razor View Engine

The Razor view engine is a view engine used in ASP.NET to generate HTML markup from views. Views are .cshtml files that define the presentation layer of your application.

ASP.NET uses Razor as the default view engine, on the other hand, Node.js another platform for building web applications is more flexibility in choosing various view engines. Some of the popular view engines for Node.js include: Pug, EJS, Handlebars, Mustache and more

Razor syntax

Razor syntax is a markup syntax. The @ symbol is used to indicate the beginning of Razor code within an HTML file.

Razor reserved keywords

Razor has a set of reserved keywords that have specific meanings in the language. These keywords cannot be used as identifiers (such as variable names, function names, etc.) because they are part of the language syntax.

case, do, default, for, foreach, if, else, lock, switch, try, catch, finally, using, while

page, namespace, functions, inherits, model, section, helper

Implicit expressions

Implicit Razor expressions start with @ followed by C# code

```
<label>@DateTime.Now</label>
```

To escape an @ symbol, use a second @ symbol:

```
<label>@@Hello</label>
```

The code is rendered in HTML with a single @ symbol

when using **await** keyword, implicit expressions must not contain spaces. If the C# statement has a clear ending, spaces can be intermingled

```
<label>@await Logic()</label>
```

Implicit expressions cannot contain generics, because the characters inside the brackets <> are interpreted as an HTML.

This code is not valid:

```
<label>@Logic<long>()</label>
```

Comments

You can include comments within your Razor markup. Use **@*** to start the comment block and ***@** to end it. Comments in Razor are a helpful way to document your code, clarify your intentions, or temporarily disable code without removing it. They are ignored by the Razor engine when generating the output, so they don't impact the rendered HTML or C# code.

```
@* <label>Hi</label>*@
```

Explicit Razor expressions

Explicit Razor expressions consist of an @ symbol with balanced parenthesis.

```
<label>@(DateTime.Now.Day + 1)</label>
```

Code blocks

Code blocks start with @ and are enclosed by {}. Unlike expressions, the C# code inside code blocks isn't rendered.

```
@{
    int num = 1;

    string GetString()
    {
        return "2";
    }
}

<label>@num</label>
<label>@GetString()</label>

@{
    num = 3;
}
```

Implicit transitions

Razor block can transition back to HTML:

```
@{
    int num = 123;
    <label>@num</label>
}
```

only '<label>123</label>' is rendered.

Render outside html tag

Explicit delimited transition with the <mark><text></mark> razor tag:

```
@{
    string name = "Eldar";
    <text>Name: @name</text>
}
```

Only 'Name: Eldar' is rendered.

Explicit line transition with <mark>@:</mark> prefix:

```
@{
    string name = "Eldar";
    @:Name: @name
}
```

Only 'Name: Eldar' is rendered.

Directives

Directives used in Razor Views contribute to adding additional functionality to the page.

page

@page: This directive is used in Razor Pages to specify the route associated with the page. It defines the URL at which the Razor Page can be accessed.

```
@page "/myPage"
```

Browser:

https://localhost:7172/myPage

model

@model: This directive specifies the model class that the Razor view is strongly typed to. It allows you to access properties and methods of the specified model within the view.

```
@model IndexModel
```

```
@Model.
    BadRequest
    Challenge
    Content
    Countries
```

using

@using: This directive imports namespaces, making their types accessible within the view. You can include multiple @using directives to access types from different namespaces.

```
@using Microsoft.AspNetCore.Mvc;
```

functions

@functions: Defines C# functions, methods, properties, and variables within a View. It allows you to encapsulate server-side code.

```
@functions {

    int Add(int x, int y)
    {
        return x + y;
    }

}

<label>@Add(1,2)</label>
```

attribute

@attribute: Used to apply attributes to Razor page.

```
@{
  @attribute [Authorize]
  string GetString()
  {
    return "Hi";
  }
}
```

implements

@implements: Used to specify that a Razor view implements a particular interface.

```
interface IMyInterface
{
    void MyMethod();
}
```

```
@implements IMyInterface

@functions {

  public void MyMethod()
  {

  }
}
```

inject

@inject: Used to inject services or dependencies into your Razor page or view.

```
public class MyLogic
{
  public string GetString()
```

```
    {
        return "Hi";
    }
}
```

```
@inject MyLogic myLogic

<label>@myLogic.GetString()</label>
```

layout

@layout: Used to specify the layout for a Razor page. The layout is a shared template or master page that defines the common structure and elements (such as headers, footers, and navigation) for multiple pages

_Layout.cshtml

```
<!DOCTYPE html>
<html>
<head> <meta charset="utf-8" /> </head>
<body>
   <div>layout header</div> @RenderBody() <div>layout footer</div>
</body>
</html>
```

Index.cshtml

```
@{ Layout = "~/Pages/Shared/_Layout.cshtml"; }


<div>page</div>
```

Browser Result

layout header

page

layout footer

Rendered HTML

```
<!DOCTYPE html>
<html>
<head> <meta charset="utf-8" /> </head>
<body>
   <div>layout header</div>
   <div>page</div>
   <div>layout footer</div>
</body>
</html>
```

You have a layout defined in the _Layout.cshtml file, and an Index.cshtml page that specifies the layout to be used. The layout contains a header, a footer, and a @RenderBody() call to render the content of the page.

namespace

@namespace: Used within Razor views for organizing and referencing classes, functions, or other elements.

```
@namespace MyNameSpace.Pages
```

section

@section: Used for defining named sections within a layout file. Child views can populate these sections with content.

Index.cshtml

```
@{
    Layout = "~/Pages/Shared/_Layout.cshtml";
}

@section Styles {
  <style>
    .myClass{ color: red; }
  </style>
}

@section Scripts {
  <script>
    function myFunction() {}
  </script>
}
```

_Layout.cshtml

```
<!DOCTYPE html>
<html>
<head>
    @await RenderSectionAsync("Styles", required: false)
</head>
<body>
    @RenderBody()
```

```
    @await RenderSectionAsync("Scripts", required: false)
</body>
</html>
```

Rendered HTML

```
<!DOCTYPE html>
<html>
<head>
    <style> .myClass {  color: red; } </style>
</head>
<body>
    <script>  function myFunction() {} </script>
</body>
</html>
```

As shown in the rendered HTML, the content defined within the "Styles" section is included in the <head> section of the HTML, and the content of the "Scripts" section is included just before the closing </body> tag. This allows you to manage and organize your styles and scripts within different views while maintaining a consistent layout structure for your web pages.

ViewImports

The _ViewImports.cshtml file is a special Razor view file that contains directives and namespaces that are automatically applied to all views within the same folder and its subfolders. It serves as a central location for specifying common settings, tag helpers, and namespaces that you want to make available in multiple views without having to repeat them in each individual view file.

```
@using EldarMVC
@using EldarMVC.Models
@addTagHelper *, Microsoft.AspNetCore.Mvc.TagHelpers
```

ViewStart

The _ViewStart.cshtml file is another special Razor view file. The _ViewStart.cshtml file is used to specify layout pages and shared layout code for a specific folder and its subfolders within the Views directory.

```
@{ Layout = "_Layout"; }
<div>1234</div>
```

ViewImports vs ViewStart

_ViewStart.cshtml contains layout-related code and HTML that is common to all views.

_ViewImports.cshtml contains directives, namespaces, tag helpers, and other common settings that apply to all views.

If you try putting HTML and layout-related code in _ViewImports.cshtml, it will not work.

If you try putting directives, namespaces, or tag helpers in _ViewStart.cshtml, it will not work.

Tag Helpers

Tag Helpers are a feature that allows you to use server-side C# code to generate HTML elements in your Razor views. They are designed to make it easier to create dynamic and reusable HTML elements by encapsulating complex logic and behavior within HTML tags. Tag Helpers look like HTML elements but are processed on the server before rendering the HTML.

Add Tag Helper

```
public class IndexModel
{
    public string MyString;
}
```

```
@model IndexModel
@addTagHelper *, Microsoft.AspNetCore.Mvc.TagHelpers

<label asp-for="@Model.MyString"></label>
```

The **@addTagHelper** directive include Tag Helpers from the "Microsoft.AspNetCore.Mvc.TagHelpers" namespace.

The **asp-for** Tag Helper is used to bind the input element to a specific model property.

Rendered HTML

```
<input type="text" id="MyString" name="MyString" value="">
```

Remove Tag Helper

@removeTagHelper: Used to exclude or remove a specific Tag Helper from being active in a Razor view. It's typically used to prevent a particular Tag Helper from applying its logic to elements within that view.

```
@removeTagHelper *, Microsoft.AspNetCore.Mvc.TagHelpers
```

Tag Helper Prefix

@tagHelperPrefix: Used to specify a prefix for Tag Helpers. This prefix is applied to Tag Helper elements within the view, allowing you to distinguish them from regular HTML elements and helping to avoid naming conflicts.

```
@tagHelperPrefix my-

<my-input asp-for="@Model.MyString">
```

Disable a Tag Helper at the element level

You can disable a Tag Helper at the element level by using the Tag Helper opt-out character, which is an exclamation mark (!). This is also known as Tag Helper suppression. When you prepend an element with !, it tells Razor to treat that element as regular HTML and not apply any Tag Helper processing to it.

```
<!input asp-for="@Model.MyString">
```

Custom Tag Helpers

You can create your own custom Tag Helpers to encapsulate complex behavior. This can be useful for creating reusable components or simplifying complex tasks.

```csharp
namespace EldarSite
{
    [HtmlTargetElement("eldar")]
    public class EldarTagHelper : TagHelper
    {
        [HtmlAttributeName("my-attribute")]
        public string MyAttribute { get; set; }

        public override async Task ProcessAsync(TagHelperContext context,
                                    TagHelperOutput output)
        {
            output.TagName = "div";
            output.Attributes.SetAttribute("class", "my-class");
            var content = await output.GetChildContentAsync();
```

```
        output.Content.SetContent($"{MyAttribute} {content.GetContent()}dar");
    }
  }
}
```

```
@addTagHelper *, EldarSite

<eldar my-attribute="Hi" >el</eldar>
```

```
<div class="my-class">Hi eldar</div>
```

In this example, the custom Tag Helper, EldarTagHelper, generates a <div> element with a class "my-class." It also allows you to set a custom attribute "my-attribute" to pass data to the Tag Helper from your Razor view.

Suppress Output

To Ignore rendering tag helper, use SuppressOutput function.

```
[HtmlTargetElement("eldar")]
 public class EldarTagHelper : TagHelper
{
    public override async Task ProcessAsync(TagHelperContext context,
                            TagHelperOutput output)
    {
        output.SuppressOutput();
    }
}
```

Html Helpers

HTML Helpers are controls and server-side components that allow you to generate HTML elements with a more declarative and server-side approach. HTML Helpers are the older approach to server-side components that existed before Tag Helpers. Most of them are no longer in use. Tag Helpers are a more modern and more readable way to generate HTML elements within your views

```
@Html.
```
- ActionLink
- AntiForgeryToken
- BeginForm
- BeginRouteForm
- CheckBox
- CheckBoxFor
- CheckBoxFor<>
- Display
- DisplayFor<>

@Html.Label

@Html.Label is a helper method used to generate an HTML label element.

```
@Html.Label("Hi")
```

Rendered HTML

```html
<label for="Hi">Hi</label>
```

@Html.Raw

@Html.Raw is a helper method that allows you to output raw HTML content to the view without HTML encoding. By default, when you output content in a Razor view using @, the content is HTML-encoded to prevent cross-site scripting (XSS) attacks.

```
@{
    string str = "<div>Eldar</div>";
}


@str


@Html.Raw(str)
```

Rendered html

```
&lt;div&gt;Eldar&lt;/div&gt;


<div>Eldar</div>
```

browser

```
<div>Eldar</div>

Eldar
```

@str: When you use @ to output a variable in Razor syntax, it automatically HTML-encodes the content. In this case, it will display the string as it is, but HTML tags will be rendered as text, not as markup.

@Html.Raw(str): This method is used to output raw HTML content without HTML encoding. It will render the HTML tags as actual markup.

Partial views

Partial views allow you to break down the user interface of a web page into smaller, reusable components. These components are essentially small views that can be rendered within other views or pages. Use the tag <partial> to include a partial view.

page.cshtml

```
<partial name="~/Views/_header.cshtml" />
<label>body</label>
<partial name="~/Views/_footer.cshtml" model="@("footer")" />
```

_header.cshtml

```
<label>header</label>
```

_footer.cshtml

```
@model string

<label>@Model</label>
```

Rendered HTML

```
<label>header</label>
<label>body</label>
<label>footer</label>
```

RenderPartialAsync

@Html.RenderPartialAsync is a method that allows you to render a partial view asynchronously within a Razor view. It is commonly used to include and render a partial view in a non-blocking way, which can improve the overall performance and responsiveness of your web application.

```
@await Html.RenderPartialAsync("_PartialName", model)
```

Partial

The Partial method is used to render a partial view and return the rendered HTML as a string. This rendered HTML can be captured and assigned to a variable within the parent view or used in other ways, such as displaying it inside a specific HTML element.

```
@{
    IHtmlContent view = Html.Partial("~/Views/_header.cshtml");
    using (var writer = new StringWriter())
    {
        view.WriteTo(writer, HtmlEncoder.Default);
        string htmlString = writer.ToString();
    }
}
```

```
string htmlString = writer.ToString();
```
htmlString   Q View ▾ "<label>header</label>"

View Components

View components are a way to render reusable, self-contained components within your views. View components are similar to partial views. View Components do not use model binding as regular views do. Instead, they rely on data passed explicitly when invoking the view component.

AdViewComponent.cs

```csharp
public class AdViewComponent : ViewComponent
{
    public async Task<IViewComponentResult> InvokeAsync(string str)
    {
        return View("AdViewComponent", str);
    }
}
```

If you want synchronous use

```csharp
public IViewComponentResult Invoke(string str)
{
    return View("AdViewComponent", str);
}
```

AdViewComponent.cshtml

```cshtml
@model string
<div>@Model</div>
```

Login.cshtml

Call the component:

```cshtml
@await Component.InvokeAsync("Ad","Hi")
```

A View Component can be invoked also as a Tag Helper :

```html
<vc:ad str="Hi"></vc:ad>
```

HTML Rendered

```
<div>Hi</div>
```

[NonViewComponent]

If you want to exclude certain classes from being treated as view components by the default view component discovery mechanism, use the NonViewComponent Attribute.

```
[NonViewComponent]
public class AdViewComponent : ViewComponent
```

Ip

An IP address (Internet Protocol address) is a numerical label assigned to each device connected to a computer network that uses the Internet Protocol for communication. IP addresses are used to identify and locate devices on a network. There are two main types of IP addresses:

IPv4 (Internet Protocol version 4): These are 32-bit numerical addresses, usually represented in the format of four decimal numbers separated by periods, like "192.168.1.1". IPv4 addresses are running out due to the increasing number of devices connected to the internet.

IPv6 (Internet Protocol version 6): These are 128-bit numerical addresses, represented in a hexadecimal format, such as "2001:0db8:85a3:0000:0000:8a2e:0370:7334". IPv6 was introduced to address the limited availability of IPv4 addresses.

Domain

A domain is a human-readable, textual representation of an internet address. It is used to identify and locate resources on the internet, such as websites. Domains are used to make it easier for people to access websites and services by providing a name that is more user-friendly than a numerical IP address. Domains are hierarchical, with the top-level domain (TLD) on the right (e.g., .com, .org) and the specific domain name on the left (e.g., example.com).

For example, "www.example.com" is a domain name.

DNS

The relationship between domains and IP addresses is established through the Domain Name System (DNS). When you enter a domain name (e.g., www.example.com) into a web browser, the DNS system is used to resolve that domain name to the corresponding IP address (e.g., 192.0.2.1), which is the actual address where the website is hosted. This process allows users to access websites using human-readable domain names while the internet uses IP addresses for routing and communication.

Port

A port is identified by a 16-bit unsigned integer, which can range from 0 to 65535. Ports are categorized into three ranges:

Well-known ports (0-1023): Reserved for system services and applications that are widely used and standardized. For example, HTTP typically uses port 80, and HTTPS uses port 443.

Registered ports (1024-49151): Reserved for applications and services that are not as widely used as well-known ports but are still standardized.

Dynamic or private ports (49152-65535): Available for temporary or private use, such as client applications that need to communicate with servers using unique port numbers.

Protocol: Port numbers are associated with a specific protocol, such as TCP (Transmission Control Protocol) or UDP (User Datagram Protocol). TCP and UDP are two of the most common transport layer protocols used in networking.

Socket: A socket is a combination of an IP address and a port number, and it represents an endpoint for network communication. Sockets are used to establish connections between devices and are crucial for network programming.

Firewalls: Ports play a significant role in firewall configuration. Firewalls can allow or block traffic based on the source and destination port numbers, helping to control network access and enhance security.

Port Scanning: Port scanning is a technique used by network administrators and security professionals to discover open ports on a target system. This can help in assessing the security of a network and identifying potential vulnerabilities.

Common Ports: Some well-known port numbers and their associated services include:

Port 80: HTTP (Hypertext Transfer Protocol)

Port 443: HTTPS (HTTP Secure)

Port 21: FTP (File Transfer Protocol)

Port 22: SFTP (Secure File Transfer Protocol)

Port 25: SMTP (Simple Mail Transfer Protocol)

SFTP

SFTP, which stands for Secure File Transfer Protocol or SSH File Transfer Protocol, is a network protocol used for securely transferring files and managing file systems over a secure channel. SFTP is an extension of the SSH (Secure Shell) protocol and provides a secure way to transfer files between a client and a server.

SMTP

SMTP, which stands for Simple Mail Transfer Protocol, is a widely used network protocol for sending and relaying email messages over the internet. It is a core component of the email infrastructure and is responsible for routing, delivering, and exchanging email messages between email clients, email servers, and other devices. Here are some key aspects of SMTP

TCP

TCP, which stands for Transmission Control Protocol, is one of the core protocols of the Internet Protocol (IP) suite. It operates at the transport layer of the OSI (Open Systems Interconnection) model and plays a crucial role in facilitating reliable, connection-oriented communication between devices over IP networks.

UDP

UDP, which stands for User Datagram Protocol, is a transport layer protocol in the Internet Protocol (IP) suite. It provides a lightweight, connectionless, and unreliable method for transmitting data between devices over IP networks.

HTTP

Hypertext Transfer Protocol (HTTP), is the foundation of data communication on the World Wide Web. It is an application layer protocol used for transmitting data between a web server and a web client, typically a web browser. ASP.NET implements the HTTP protocol. Here are some key points about HTTP:

Stateless Protocol

HTTP is a stateless protocol, meaning that each request from a client to a server is treated independently, without any knowledge of previous requests.

Request-Response Model

HTTP operates on a request-response model. A client, typically a web browser, sends an HTTP request to a web server, which processes the request and sends back an HTTP response. The request and response contain information about the resource being requested, the desired operation (e.g., GET, POST, PUT, DELETE), and various headers for communication and negotiation.

URLs

URLs (Uniform Resource Locators) are used to specify the resource being requested. A URL typically includes the protocol (http:// or https://), domain (e.g., www.example.com), and path to the resource (e.g., /page).

Query string

A query string is a component of a URL (Uniform Resource Locator) that is used to pass data or parameters to a web server when making an HTTP request. It is typically placed at the end of the URL and consists of a question mark (?) followed by a series of key-value pairs separated by ampersands (&).

URL - https://localhost:7223/home/login?email=eldar@g.com&password=1234

Base Url - https://localhost:7223

Path - /home/login

? - marks the beginning of the query string.

Key-Value Pairs within the query string - email=eldar@g.com, password=1234

& - A delimiter to separate multiple key-value pairs or parameters

HTTP Methods

HTTP defines several methods (also known as verbs) that describe the action to be performed on a resource

GET: Used to request data from a specified resource.

POST: Used to submit data to be processed to a specified resource.

PUT: Used to update or replace an existing resource.

PATCH: Used to apply partial modifications to a resource.

DELETE: Used to request the removal of a resource.

HEAD: The HEAD method is similar to GET but is used to request the headers of a resource without receiving the actual resource content.

OPTIONS: Used to retrieve information about the communication options for the target resource. It returns a description of the communication options available for the resource, such as which HTTP methods are supported.

CONNECT: Used for establishing network connections to a resource, typically for proxy-related communication. It is not widely used in standard web applications.

TRACE: Used to perform a message loop-back test along the path to the target resource. It is used for diagnostic and debugging purposes, allowing a client to see how a request changes as it passes through intermediaries (e.g., proxy servers).

Status Codes

HTTP responses include status codes to indicate the outcome of the request. Common status codes include:

Status Code	Description
200 OK	The request was successful and the server has sent back the requested data.
201 Created	The request was successful and the server has created a new resource.
202 Accepted	The request was successful and the server has accepted the request, but the processing is not yet complete.
400 Bad Request	The request was invalid.
401 Unauthorized	The client is not authorized to access the requested resource.
403 Forbidden	The client is forbidden to access the requested resource.
404 Not Found	The requested resource could not be found.
500 Internal Server Error	An unexpected error occurred on the server.
502 Bad Gateway	The server received an invalid response from an upstream server.
503 Service Unavailable	The server is currently unavailable.

Headers

HTTP requests and responses include headers, which contain metadata about the request or response. Headers can convey information about the content type, content length, caching, and more.

HTTPS

HTTPS (HyperText Transfer Protocol Secure) is simply HTTP over TLS (Transport Layer Security) (or formerly, over SSL). This means that the HTTP protocol is used as usual, but all communication is encrypted and protected by the underlying TLS layer, ensuring confidentiality, integrity, and authenticity of the data exchanged between client and server..

Cookies

HTTP supports the use of cookies, which are small pieces of data stored on the client's side and sent with each request. Cookies are often used for session management, user authentication, and tracking user preferences.

HTTP requests are made up of the following components

Request line: The request line specifies the method, request URI, and HTTP version. The method is the action that the client wants the server to perform, such as GET, POST, or PUT. The request URI is the identity of the resource that the client wants to retrieve. The HTTP version is the version of the HTTP protocol that the client is using.

Request headers: Request headers contain additional information about the request, such as the client's browser type and the content type of the requested resource.

Request body: The request body may contain data that the client is sending to the server, such as form data or a file.

HTTP responses are made up of the following components:

Status line: The status line specifies the HTTP version, the status code, and a reason phrase. The status code is a number that indicates the outcome of the request. The most common status codes are 200 (OK), 404 (Not Found), and 500 (Internal Server Error).

Response headers: Response headers contain additional information about the response, such as the content type of the response body and the length of the response body.

Response body: The response body contains the data that the server is sending to the client.

Requests and responses with http protocol examples

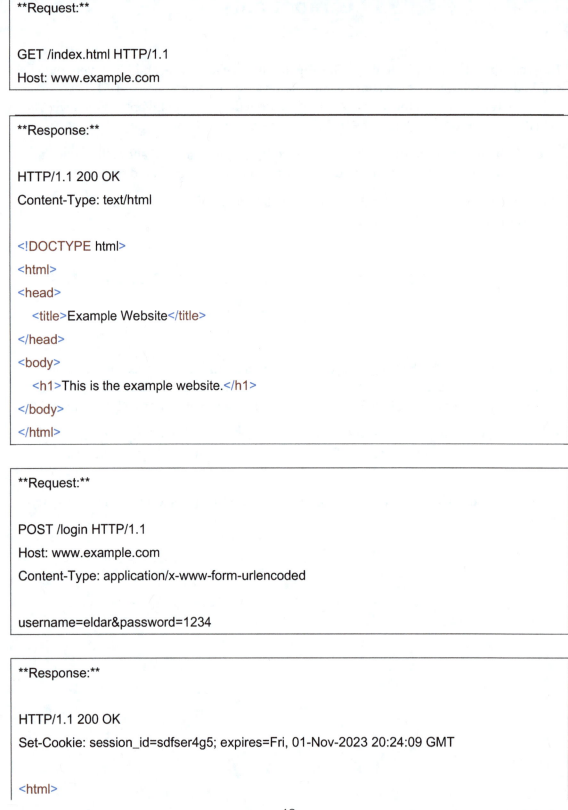

Request:

GET /index.html HTTP/1.1

Host: www.example.com

Response:

HTTP/1.1 200 OK

Content-Type: text/html

```html
<!DOCTYPE html>
<html>
<head>
  <title>Example Website</title>
</head>
<body>
  <h1>This is the example website.</h1>
</body>
</html>
```

Request:

POST /login HTTP/1.1

Host: www.example.com

Content-Type: application/x-www-form-urlencoded

username=eldar&password=1234

Response:

HTTP/1.1 200 OK

Set-Cookie: session_id=sdfser4g5; expires=Fri, 01-Nov-2023 20:24:09 GMT

```html
<html>
```

```html
<head>
  <title>Login Successful</title>
</head>
<body>
  <h1>You are now logged in.</h1>
</body>
</html>
```

HTTP Support Formats

HTTP is a protocol used for transferring data, it is content-agnostic, which means it does not restrict the type of data that can be transferred. Instead, HTTP relies on the use of specific headers, such as "Content-Type," to specify the format of the data being sent. Here are three common formats that HTTP can support:

HTML (Hypertext Markup Language): HTML is the standard markup language used for creating web pages. When a server responds to an HTTP request with a "Content-Type" header set to "text/html," the client (typically a web browser) interprets the received data as HTML and renders it as a web page.

XML (Extensible Markup Language): XML is a versatile markup language that can be used to represent structured data. HTTP can support XML by specifying a "Content-Type" header of "application/xml" or "text/xml" in the response. This informs the client that the data being transferred is in XML format.

JSON (JavaScript Object Notation): JSON is a lightweight data interchange format that is commonly used in web applications for sending and receiving structured data. HTTP can support JSON by specifying a "Content-Type" header of "application/json" in the response. This signals to the client that the data is in JSON format.

In addition to HTML, XML, and JSON, HTTP can support various other content types, including images, videos, plain text, binary data, and custom formats, by specifying the appropriate "Content-Type" in the HTTP response headers. The ability to transmit different content types makes HTTP a versatile protocol for transferring a wide range of data over the internet.

Send data

When sending data in an HTTP request, you have two common options: sending data in the URL (as query parameters) or sending data in the request body. The choice between these methods depends on the type of data, the size of the data, and the HTTP method you are.

URL Limitations

Length: URLs have a maximum length limit, which varies depending on web browsers, servers, and other factors. For practical purposes, URLs are typically limited to a few thousand characters. Extremely long URLs can cause issues with certain web servers.

Character Encoding: URLs can only contain a limited set of characters, mainly alphanumeric characters, hyphens, underscores, and a few special characters like the question mark and the equal sign. Other characters must be URL-encoded.

Browser Limits: Different web browsers may have their own limits on URL length, and these limits may vary. For example, Internet Explorer has a limit of 2,083 characters for URL length.

HTTP Request/Response Body Limitations

Request Body Size: The size of an HTTP request body is not strictly defined by the HTTP/1.1 specification, but it can be limited by various factors, including the web server, the client, and any intermediate proxies or firewalls. In practice, most servers and clients have configuration settings to limit request body size to prevent abuse.

Response Body Size: Similar to request bodies, response body size can be limited by the server, client, and network infrastructure. Some servers may also implement response size limits to prevent excessive resource consumption.

Chunked Encoding: Chunked Transfer Encoding allows for streaming of data, where the size of each chunk can be limited. This enables processing of large request/response bodies in smaller, manageable pieces.

URL encoding

URL encoding, also known as percent encoding, is a method used to represent special characters and non-ASCII characters within a URL (Uniform Resource Locator). URLs cannot contain certain characters directly, such as spaces or non-ASCII characters, because they may have special meanings or cause parsing issues. URL encoding replaces these characters with a "%" symbol followed by two hexadecimal digits that represent the character's ASCII code.

Here are the steps for URL encoding:

1. Convert Character to ASCII: Determine the ASCII code of the character that needs to be encoded. For example, the ASCII code for the space character is 32.

2. Convert ASCII to Hexadecimal: Convert the ASCII code to its hexadecimal representation. For example, 32 in decimal is 20 in hexadecimal.

3. Prefix with %: Precede the hexadecimal representation with a "%" symbol. In this example, 20 becomes "%20".

Commonly encoded characters include spaces, ampersands ("&"), question marks ("?"), equals signs ("="), and non-ASCII characters like accented letters. Here are a few examples of URL encoding:

Space character: Encoded as "%20"

Ampersand ("&"): Encoded as "%26"

Question mark ("?"): Encoded as "%3F"

Equals sign ("="): Encoded as "%3D"

Non-ASCII character "é": Encoded as "%C3%A9" (UTF-8 representation)

This code demonstrates how to encode a string and then decode it

```
string originalString = "& special !";
string encodedString = Uri.EscapeDataString(originalString);
Console.WriteLine(encodedString); // %26%20special%20!


string encodedString2 =UrlEncoder.Default.Encode(originalString);
Console.WriteLine(encodedString2); // %26%20special%20%21


string decodedString = Uri.UnescapeDataString(encodedString);
Console.WriteLine(decodedString);// & special !
```

In ASP.NET, when you work with parameters in controllers, URL encoding and decoding typically happen automatically for you. ASP.NET handles the encoding and decoding of values in routes, query parameters, and form data to ensure that data is correctly transmitted and interpreted. This helps prevent issues related to special characters and URL safety.

REST

REST (Representational State Transfer), is an architectural style for designing networked applications. It is not a protocol but a set of principles and constraints that guide the design of web services and APIs.

REST does not specify the use of HTTP, but it is commonly associated with HTTP due to the widespread use of HTTP for web-based communication.

When people refer to "RESTful" services or APIs, they are usually describing web services that follow REST principles and use HTTP as the underlying communication protocol.

In a RESTful context, HTTP methods (GET, POST, PUT, DELETE) are used to interact with resources (identified by URIs) in a manner that aligns with REST constraints.

REST emphasizes stateless communication, where each client request to the server is independent, and the server does not maintain any client-specific state between requests.

SOAP

Simple Object Access Protocol (SOAP), is a protocol for exchanging structured information in the implementation of web services. It is one of the traditional and widely used methods for enabling communication between different software applications, typically over the internet.

XML-Based: SOAP messages are typically formatted using XML (eXtensible Markup Language).

SOAP messages can be transmitted over various transport protocols, including HTTP, SMTP, TCP, and more. However, it is most commonly used over HTTP, making it suitable for web services.

A SOAP message consists of an envelope that contains the header and body elements. The header can carry metadata and additional information about the message, while the body contains the actual data being exchanged.

SOAP is based on a set of well-defined and widely accepted standards, including WSDL (Web Services Description Language) for describing web services, UDDI (Universal Description, Discovery, and Integration) for service discovery, and others.

SOAP is considered an older technology in the context of web services and API development. It was widely used in the early 2000s and was a popular choice for building enterprise-level and distributed systems. While SOAP is still used in some legacy systems and industries that require strict standards and reliability, it has become less common in modern web development, where alternatives like REST (Representational State Transfer) and JSON (JavaScript Object Notation) have gained widespread adoption.

MVC

ASP.NET MVC (Model-View-Controller) is a web development framework provided by Microsoft for building web applications. It separates the application logic into three interconnected components: Model, View, and Controller.

Model: The Model is a class that contains the data. Some developers place the logic responsible for populating the data within the model, while others separate this logic into another component called logic.

View: The View is a CSHTML Razor page that takes the model and builds the view.

Controller: The Controller handles user input, processes requests, and manages the communication between the Model and the View. Some developers use the controller as a logic component instead of the model.

Create new project

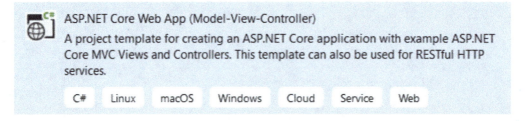

Expected Solution:

Show data and send data include fields validation

LoginModel.cs

```csharp
using System.ComponentModel.DataAnnotations;

namespace EldarMVC.Models.Home
{
    public class LoginModel
    {
        [Required, EmailAddress, StringLength(150)]
        public string Email { get; set; }

        [Required, StringLength(20)]
        public string Password { get; set; }

        public string? Message { get; set; }
    }
}
```

Data annotations validation attributes

[Required] attribute: indicates that a value for this property is required.

[EmailAddress] attribute: ensures that the value is a valid email address.

[StringLength(150)] attribute: specifies that the maximum length of the email address should be 150 characters.

```
namespace EldarMVC.Controllers
{
    public class HomeController : Controller
    {
        [HttpGet]
        public IActionResult Login()
        {
            return View(new LoginModel());
        }


        [HttpPost]
        public IActionResult Login(LoginModel login)
        {
            if (ModelState.IsValid)
            {
                // login logic
                login.Message = "Success";
            }
            else
            {
                login.Message = "Failed";
            }
            return View(login);
        }
    }
}
```

A controller is used to group a set of actions. An action is a method on a controller which handles requests.

[HttpGet]: This attribute is applied to the Login action method to specify that it should handle HTTP GET requests. In other words, this method will be executed when a user navigates to the login page.

View(new LoginModel()): This line passes the LoginModel instance to the view. The "Login" action is associated with a view named "Login". The view is expected to be located in a folder named after the controller "Home" within the "Views" folder.

IActionResult: used to represent the result of an action method and encapsulate the response that will be sent to the client.

[HttpPost]: This attribute is applied to the Login action method to specify that it should handle HTTP POST requests. This method will be executed when the user submits login form.

ModelState: Used to store model state information, including validation errors. **ModelState.IsValid**: Checks if there are any validation errors according to the validation attributes. If there are no errors, it indicates that the form data passed validation rules.

Login.cshtml

```
@using EldarMVC.Models.Home;
@model LoginModel


<form asp-action="Login" asp-controller="Home" method="post">
  <div class="form-group">
    <label asp-for="@Model.Email"></label>
    <input asp-for="@Model.Email" class="form-control" />
    <span asp-validation-for="@Model.Email"
      class="text-danger"></span>
  </div>
  <div class="form-group">
    <label asp-for="@Model.Password"></label>
    <input asp-for="@Model.Password" class="form-control" />
    <span asp-validation-for="@Model.Password"
      class="text-danger"></span>
  </div>
  <button type="submit" class="btn btn-primary">Submit</button>
<div>
  @Model.Message
</div>
</form>
```

Form attributes:

asp-action="Login": Tag helpers that specifies that the form should be submitted to the "Login" action of the specified controller.

asp-controller="Home": Tag helpers that specifies the name of the controller to which the form submission should be directed.

method="post": indicates that the form should be submitted using the HTTP POST method. This is commonly used for form submissions that modify data on the server.

Form inside fields attributes:

asp-for: Tag helpers that specify the model property that you want to bind to.

asp-validation-for: Tag helpers that used for client-side and server-side validation in forms. It's to display validation error messages next to form fields.

button: When the user clicks this button, it triggers the form's submission.

Browser	**After clicking the button**

localhost:7223/Home/Login

Email

Password

Submit

Email

The Email field is required.
Password

The Password field is required.
Submit

Failed

After clicking the submit button with invalid values, we can see in the image the invalid fields stored inside the **ModelState** object.

```
[HttpPost]
0 references
public IActionResult Login(LoginModel login)
{
    if (ModelState.IsValid)
    {
        //
        log
    }
    else
    {
        log
    }
    return
}
```

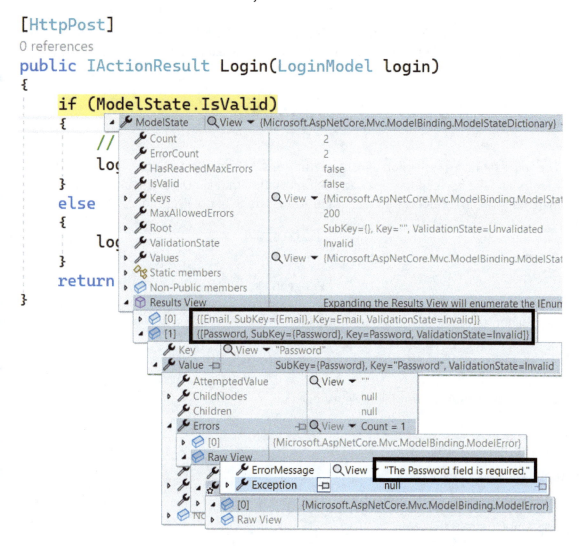

Enter valid data and click submit

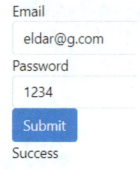

Email

eldar@g.com

Password

1234

Submit

Success

Routing

MVC routing is the process of determining how incoming HTTP requests should be handled and which controller action method should be executed.

Route Table

The route table is a collection of route definitions. Each route definition specifies a URL pattern and the corresponding controller and action that should be invoked when a matching URL is received. Route configuration is done in the Program.cs file.

Pattern

Progran.cs

```
var builder = WebApplication.CreateBuilder(args);

//Add MVC services to the application.
builder.Services.AddControllersWithViews();

var app = builder.Build();
app.UseStaticFiles();
app.UseRouting();
app.MapControllerRoute(
    name: "default",
```

```
//Route pattern
pattern: "{controller}/{action}");
app.Run();
```

Default pattern defines a default route for your application.

Pattern: ControllerName/ActionName

If the user visits a URL " https://localhost:7223/Home/Login," it will map to the "Login" action within the "Home" controller.

In MVC, if you create a controller class with a name ending in "Controller," it will be automatically included in the routing system as part of the route.

Default Route

The default route is a predefined routing pattern that is used when no specific route matches an incoming URL.

```
app.MapControllerRoute(
    name: "default",
    //Route pattern
    pattern: "{controller=Home}/{action=Login}");
```

{controller=Home}: Default controller is Home

{action=Login}: Default action is Login

Now all the URLs below will redirect to login view:

https://localhost:7223

https://localhost:7223/home

Route Parameters

Routes can include placeholders called route parameters, which are enclosed in curly braces {}. These parameters can capture values from the URL and pass them as arguments to the controller action methods.

```
app.MapControllerRoute(
    name: "default",
    //Route pattern
    pattern: "{controller=Home}/{action=Login}/{id?}");
```

{id?}: The "id" parameter is marked with a question mark, indicating that it's optional. This means that a URL doesn't have to include an "id" parameter, but if it does, it will be captured as part of the route.

```
[HttpGet]
0 references
public IActionResult Login(string id)
{                                          id    View ▼ "1234"
    return View(new LoginModel());    ≤ 6ms elapsed
}
```

Route Constraints

Route constraints are used to restrict which routes match a URL pattern based on criteria such as data type, regular expressions, or custom logic. Constraints ensure that the routing engine selects the correct route for a given URL.

```
app.MapControllerRoute(
    name: "default",
    //Route pattern
    pattern: "{controller=Home}/{action=Login}/{id:int?}");
```

:int constrains a route parameter to be an integer.

If the user visits a URL https://localhost:7223/home/login/abc it will cause error not found page.

Areas

In larger MVC applications, areas are used to organize controllers and views into logical groups. Each area can have its own set of routes, allowing for better organization and separation of concerns.

Add to program.file:

```
app.MapAreaControllerRoute(
    name: "default",
    areaName: "admin",
    dataTokens: new { namespaces = new[] {
                    "EldarMVC.Areas.Admin" } },
    pattern: "admin/{controller=Home}/{action=Index}");
```

dataTokens: It indicates that the controllers in the "admin" area should be looked up in the "EldarMVC.Areas.Admin" namespace.

Add Areas folder, with its own Controllers, Models and Views folders.

If the user visits a URL
https://localhost:7223/admin/home/index

 it will redirect to Index view of home controller inside admin area.

Attribute Routing

MVC also supports attribute routing, where you can define routes directly on the controller actions using attributes. This approach is more flexible and allows for more fine-grained control over routing.

```
[Route("home")]
public class HomeController : Controller
{
    [HttpGet("login")]
    public IActionResult Login(string id)
    {
        return View(new LoginModel());
    }
}
```

Add this code to program.cs file

```
app.UseEndpoints(endpoints =>
{
    endpoints.MapControllers();
});
```

Area Attribute

```
[Area("admin")]
public class HomeController : Controller
{
}
```

Minimal APIs

You can configure routes directly inside the Program.cs file. This is useful for creating simple, self-contained routes for minimal applications, or for handling specific routes separately.

```
app.MapGet("/", () => "Hello World!");
```

The example configures a route to respond to HTTP GET requests to the root URL ("/") and returns "Hello World!" as the response.

Controller class

Controllers are responsible for handling incoming HTTP requests from. Controllers are associated with specific routes or URLs. The routing system directs incoming requests to the appropriate controller action based on the URL and HTTP method. Controller classes contain action methods, which are responsible for executing specific functionality in response to a request. These methods can perform tasks such as retrieving data, processing input, and rendering views. Action methods can access data from incoming HTTP requests, such as form data, query parameters, route data, and JSON or XML payloads.

Controllers can return data to the client in various forms, such as HTML views, JSON, XML, or files.

When you inherit from Controller class, you gain access to various built-in properties and methods. These objects and members are part of the Controller class and are useful for handling HTTP requests, interacting with the Model and View components, and performing other common tasks in web development.

HttpContext

The HttpContext property allows you to access information about the current HTTP request, including request headers, parameters, and more.

```
public class HomeController : Controller
{
    0 references
    public IActionResult Login()
    {
        var c=HttpContext;
        retur[c] {Microsoft.AspNetCore.Http.DefaultHttpContext}
    }
            ▸ 🔧 Connection        {Microsoft.AspNetCore.Http.DefaultConnectionInfo}
            ▸ 🔧 Features          {Microsoft.AspNetCore.Server.Kestrel.Core.Internal.Http2.H
            ▸ 🔧 FormOptions       {Microsoft.AspNetCore.Http.Features.FormOptions}
            ▸ 🔧 HttpContext       {Microsoft.AspNetCore.Http.DefaultHttpContext}
    [HttpGet("" ▸ 🔧 Items          {Microsoft.AspNetCore.Http.ItemsDictionary}
    0 references ▸ 🔧 Request        {Microsoft.AspNetCore.Http.DefaultHttpRequest}
    public IAc ▸ 🔧 RequestAborted   IsCancellationRequested = false
    {           ▸ 🔧 RequestServices  {Microsoft.Extensions.DependencyInjection.ServiceLookup
                ▸ 🔧 Response        {Microsoft.AspNetCore.Http.DefaultHttpResponse}
        return  ▸ 🔧 ServiceScopeFactory {Microsoft.Extensions.DependencyInjection.ServiceLookup
    }           ❌ Session         '((Microsoft.AspNetCore.Http.DefaultHttpContext)c).Sessi
                   🔧 TraceIdentifier  "0HMUR09PDJP47:00000001"
    [HttpPost]  ▸ 🔧 User            {System.Security.Claims.ClaimsPrincipal}
                ▸ 🔧 WebSockets      {Microsoft.AspNetCore.Http.DefaultWebSocketManager}
```

Query string

Ways to access query string values:

URL: https://localhost:7223/home/login?email=eldar@g.com&password=1234

```csharp
public IActionResult Login()
{
    //To retrieve the entire query string as a string
    string qs = HttpContext.Request.QueryString.Value;


    //To retrieve specific parameter
    string email = HttpContext.Request.Query["email"];
    string password = HttpContext.Request.Query["password"];


    return View(new LoginModel());
}
```

Name	Value
qs	"?email=eldar@g.com&password=1234"
email	"eldar@g.com"
password	"1234"

Items

Allows you to store and access data associated with a specific HTTP request. This collection is used to share data across various components within the request processing pipeline. Data stored in Items is available only for the duration of the current HTTP request. Once the request is completed, the data in Items is no longer accessible.

```
//Storing data
HttpContext.Items["UserId"] = 123;


// Retrieving data
var userId = HttpContext.Items["UserId"];


return View(new LoginModel());
```

Headers

HTTP headers are key-value pairs sent between the client (like your browser or app) and the server in an HTTP request or response.

Read headers from request:

```
var requestHeaders = HttpContext.Request.Headers;


string userAgent = requestHeaders["User-Agent"];
string contentType = requestHeaders["Content-Type"];
```

Send header to client in response:

```
HttpContext.Response.Headers.Add("CustomHeader", "HeaderValue");
```

Examples:

Header	Direction	Purpose	Example Value
Host	Request	Domain name of server	www.example.com
User-Agent	Request	Client/browser info	Mozilla/5.0 ...
Accept	Request	What types of data client accepts	application/json
Authorization	Request	Credentials for authentication (e.g., Bearer, Basic)	Bearer abcdef...
Content-Type	Both	Type of data in body	application/json
Cookie	Request	Sent by browser, holds cookies	sessionid=abc123
Set-Cookie	Response	Server sets a cookie for browser	sessionid=abc123
Cache-Control	Response	How/if client should cache this response	no-cache
Location	Response	URL to redirect to (3xx responses)	https://...
Content-Length	Both	Size of the body in bytes	1234
X-Frame-Options	Response	Clickjacking protection	DENY

ViewData

The ViewData property is a dictionary-like object that allows you to pass data from the controller to the associated view. Data stored in ViewData is available only for the current request.

HomeController.cs

```
ViewData["Message"] = "Hello, world!";
```

Login.cshtml

```
@{
    string message = (string)ViewData["Message"];
}


<h1>@ViewData["Message"]</h1>
```

ViewBag

The ViewBag is similar to ViewData but is a dynamic object.

HomeController.cs

```
ViewBag["Message"] = "Hello, world!";
```

Login.cshtml

```
@{
    string message = ViewBag["Message"];
}


<h1>@ViewBag["Message"]</h1>
```

TempData

TempData is similar to ViewData but accessible during the next request but not beyond that. If you don't access it in the subsequent request, it will be discarded.

View/Model

The View() method is used to render a view and return it as a response. You can pass a model object to this method.

```
public class HomeController : Controller
{
    public IActionResult Login()
    {
        return View(new LoginModel());
    }
}
```

The "Login" action is associated with a view named "Login". The view is expected to be located in a folder named after the controller "Home" within the "Views" folder.

```
/ Views
    / Home
        Login.cshtml
```

You can also specify a path to a view if it's located in a different.

```
return View("~/Views/Admin/Contact.cshtml");


return View("~/Views/Admin/Contact.cshtml", new LoginModel());
```

Json

Json(): Used to return JSON data from a controller action. **JsonResult** is a specific implementation of IActionResult used to return data in JSON format as an HTTP response.

```
public JsonResult Index()
{
    var data = new
    {
        Name = "Eldar",
```

```
        Age = 30,
        Email = "eldar@g.com"
    };
    // return data as JSON
    return Json(data);
}
```

Browser result: {"name":"Eldar","age":30,"email":"eldar@g.com"}

HTTP Attributes

Attributes to specify the HTTP method for each action.

```
public class HomeController : Controller
{
    [HttpGet] public void Get() { }

    [HttpPost] public void Post() { }

    [HttpPut] public void Put() { }

    [HttpPatch] public void Patch() { }

    [HttpDelete] public void Delete() { }

    [HttpHead] public void Head() { }

    [HttpOptions] public void Options() { }
}
```

if you don't specify an HTTP method attribute above an action method, the default HTTP method for that action method is GET.

RESTful

RESTful refers to a design style or architecture that adheres to the principles and constraints of REST.

When implementing RESTful principles with MVC, it essentially means using four methods associated with the same route, and the parameter that guides the request to the correct method is the HTTP method.

```
[Route("User")]
public class UserController : Controller
{
    [HttpGet] public void Get() { }

    [HttpPost] public void Post() { }

    [HttpPut] public void Put() { }

    [HttpDelete] public void Delete() { }
}
```

In real life, most developers use GET when sending a single parameter or none and POST when sending more than one parameter, distinguishing the methods by the URL rather than the method type.

ModelState

ModelState is a component for managing the state of model binding and validation during the processing of an HTTP request.

Model Binding: When a client sends data in an HTTP request, The server attempts to bind this data to the properties of model objects. ModelState keeps track of the results of this model binding process, including binding errors and validation errors.

Validation: You can add validation rules and annotations to your model properties, such as required fields, range constraints, and regular expressions. When a model is bound, ModelState is used to store information about validation errors.

Accessing Data: You can access the data in ModelState from within your controller actions. It allows you to examine the validation state of your model, check for errors, and provide feedback to the user.

Displaying Errors: In the view, you can use ModelState to display validation errors to the user. The Html.ValidationMessageFor and Html.ValidationSummary helper methods in Razor views are often used to render error messages based on ModelState.

An example of how to bind and display errors was already shown in the 'Show data and send data including field validation section.

Server Validation

Server validation is an important aspect of web and application development. It involves validating data on the server-side before processing or storing it. Whenever your application or website receives data from users, such as form submissions, login credentials, or file uploads, you should validate this data on the server. This helps prevent malicious input, such as SQL injection, cross-site scripting (XSS), and other security vulnerabilities.

DataAnnotations

Data annotations are attributes that can be applied to model properties to specify validation rules and other metadata about the data that a model represents. These annotations are used to control how data is entered, displayed, and validated.

```
[HttpPost]
public IActionResult Login(LoginModel login)
{
    if (ModelState.IsValid)
    {

    }
    return View();
}
```

```
public class LoginModel
{
    [Required, EmailAddress]
    public string Email { get; set; }

    [Required, StringLength(20)]
    public string Password { get; set; }
}
```

Here are the data annotations that are available:

```
//used to mark a property as required
[Required]


//sets maximum and minimum lengths for a string property
[StringLength(50, MinimumLength = 3)]


//constrains a numeric property to a specific range
[Range(1, 10)]


//specifies that a string property must match a given regular expresson pattern
[RegularExpression(@"^[A-Z]+[a-zA-Z'\s]*$")]
```

```csharp
//checks if the value of one property matches another
//property's value typically used for password confirmation
[Compare("Password")]

//validates that a string is a valid email address
[EmailAddress]

//validates that a string is a valid phone number
[Phone]

//validates that a string is a valid credit card number
[CreditCard]

//array has a minimum length of 3 elements
[MinLength(3)]

//array has a maximum length of 6 elements
[MaxLength(6)]

//customize the display name. the name will appear in the
//html tag name instead the c# variable name
[Display(Name = "First Name")]

//by default, every attribute has default error message,
//you can change it with ErrorMessage field.
[Required(ErrorMessage = "Error")]

//format the value of the field for display
[DisplayFormat(DataFormatString = "{0:c}")]

//Specifies the range of acceptable values for the property. In this example, //the property's value must be
greater than 0 and less than 100. Setting //MinimumIsExclusive and MaximumIsExclusive to true makes
the range exclusive, //meaning the values 0 and 100 //themselves are not allowed.
[Range(0, 100, MinimumIsExclusive = true,
                MaximumIsExclusive = true)]

//Specifies the length constraints for string properties. In this example, the //length of the string must be
between //10 and 20 characters.
[Length(10, 20)]
```

```csharp
//Validates that the annotated property is a valid Base64-//encoded string.
[Base64String]

//Specifies a list of allowed values for the property. Only the values
//"Orange"and "Apple" are permitted.
[AllowedValues("Orange", "Apple")]

//Specifies a list of denied values for the property. Values "Admin" and //"Manager" are not allowed for the //property.
[DeniedValues("Admin", "Manager")]

//validation is performed by specifying the data type of a property.
[DataType(DataType.PostalCode)]
```

DataType enum

```
public enum DataType
{
    Custom = 0, // a custom data type.

    DateTime = 1, // an instant in time, expressed as a date and time of day.

    Date = 2, // a date value.

    Time = 3, // a time value.

    Duration = 4, // a continuous time during which an object exists.

    PhoneNumber = 5, // a phone number value.

    Currency = 6, // a currency value.

    Text = 7, // text that is displayed.

    Html = 8, // an HTML file.

    MultilineText = 9, // multi-line text.

    EmailAddress = 10, // an email address.

    Password = 11, // a password value.

    Url = 12, // a URL value.

    ImageUrl = 13, // a URL to an image.

    CreditCard = 14, // a credit card number.

    PostalCode = 15, // Represents a postal code.

    Upload = 16 // Represents file upload data type.
}
```

Client Validation

Client validation is a process in web and application development where data input is validated on the client-side, typically within the user's web browser or application, before being sent to the server for further processing. Client-side validation is essential for improving user experience and reducing the number of unnecessary server requests. Client-side validation should never be considered a replacement for server-side validation. Instead, it should complement server-side validation. Malicious users can easily bypass or tamper with client-side validation.

Server vs Client validation

Feature	Client-side validation	Server-side validation
When performed	Before the data is submitted to the server	After the data is submitted to the server
Technology used	JavaScript, other client-side technologies	C#, other server-side technologies
Advantages	Provides immediate feedback to the user, improves the user experience, reduces the load on the server	More secure, ensures that all data is validated correctly
Disadvantages	Can be bypassed by users, can be less reliable	Can add latency to the application, can increase the load on the server
Best practices	Use both client-side and server-side validation for best results	Use client-side validation for basic validations, use server-side validation for more complex validations and to ensure security and integrity

Add client-side validation

To make client-side validation work in accordance with the attributes used in the model class, you need to add 3 JavaScript libraries:

jquery.js: https://jquery.com

jquery.validate.js: https://jqueryvalidation.org

jquery.validate.unobtrusive.js: https://github.com/aspnet/jquery-validation-unobtrusive

When you create a new ASP.NET MVC project, the libraries should already be included in the project. If they are not, you can download them from the links above and add them to your project.

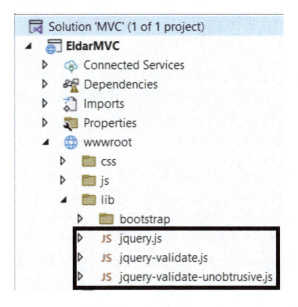

Add the files to your cshtml page or layout page if you need them to be available on every page that uses the layout page.

```
<script src="~/lib/jquery.min.js"></script>
<script src="~/lib/jquery-validate.min.js"></script>
<script src="~/lib/jquery-validate-unobtrusive.min.js"></script>
```

The order of the script tags is matters.

Now when you submit a form with invalid values, the validation will occur also in the client side with JavaScript according to the attributes used in the model class. You can test, debug the code, and submit invalid values to see that no requests are sent to the server.

Remote attribute

The Remote attribute is used for client-side remote validation. It allows you to perform validation by making an AJAX request to a server-side action method to check whether a value entered by the user in a form field is valid.

When you make a traditional HTTP request, the entire web page typically refreshes, which can result in the loss of the current page state, including input values and other user interactions. This is where AJAX (Asynchronous JavaScript and XML) comes into play. AJAX allows you to make asynchronous requests to the server, which means that you can interact with the server without reloading the entire page. Instead, you can update specific parts of the page, often referred to as "partial page updates."

When a user registers on your site, you need to check if the email is not already occupied by another user.

A function that checks if the email is not already occupied

```
[HttpPost]
public JsonResult IsEmailExist(string email)
{
    // go to database to find if email already exist
    return Json(true);
}
```

Add Remote attribute on email field

```
[Remote("IsEmailExist", "Home", HttpMethod = "POST",
                ErrorMessage = "Email already exists.")]
[Required, EmailAddress, StringLength(150)]
public string Email { get; set; }
```

"IsEmailExist": Action

"Home": Controller Name

HttpMethod = "POST": Specifies the HTTP method (POST) to be used when making the AJAX request to the server.

ErrorMessage = Specifies the error message that will be displayed to the user if the client-side validation fails.

Custom validation attribute

You can create custom validation attributes to define your own validation rules for model properties. These custom attributes allow you to add specific validation logic to ensure that data meets your application's requirements.

Create a custom validation attribute that checks whether the MyDate falls between StartDate and EndDate.

Server validation

```csharp
public class DateRangeAttribute : ValidationAttribute, IClientValidatable
{
    private readonly string startDateProperty;
    private readonly string endDateProperty;

    public DateRangeAttribute(string startDateProperty, string endDateProperty)
    {
        this.startDateProperty = startDateProperty;
        this.endDateProperty = endDateProperty;
    }

    protected override ValidationResult IsValid(object value,
                    ValidationContext validationContext)
    {
        var startDatePropertyInfo = validationContext .ObjectType
                            .GetProperty(startDateProperty);

        var endDatePropertyInfo = validationContext.ObjectType
                            .GetProperty(endDateProperty);

        if (startDatePropertyInfo == null || endDatePropertyInfo == null)
        {
            return new ValidationResult("Start or end date properties not found.");
        }

        var startDate = (DateOnly)startDatePropertyInfo
                    .GetValue(validationContext.ObjectInstance, null);
        var endDate = (DateOnly)endDatePropertyInfo
                    .GetValue(validationContext.ObjectInstance, null);
        var myDate = (DateOnly)value;
```

```csharp
        if (myDate >= startDate && myDate <= endDate)
        {
            return ValidationResult.Success;
        }

        return new ValidationResult(
                "MyDate should be between StartDate and EndDate.");
    }

    //for client validation
    public IEnumerable<ModelClientValidationRule>
            GetClientValidationRules(ModelMetadata metadata,
                        ControllerContext context)
    {


        var rule = new ModelClientValidationRule
        {
            ValidationType = "daterange",
            ErrorMessage = FormatErrorMessage(metadata.GetDisplayName())
        };
        rule.ValidationParameters.Add("startdateproperty", startDateProperty);
        rule.ValidationParameters.Add("enddateproperty", endDateProperty);
        yield return rule;
    }
}
```

Client validation

```javascript
<script>
    $.validator.addMethod("daterange", function (value, element, params)
    {
        var startDate = new Date(params.startdateproperty);
        var endDate = new Date(params.enddateproperty);
        var myDate = new Date(value);

        return myDate >= startDate && myDate <= endDate;
    });


    $.validator.unobtrusive.adapters.add("daterange", ["startdateproperty",
```

89

```
                          "enddateproperty"], function (options) {
      options.rules["daterange"] = options.params;
      options.messages["daterange"] = options.message;
   });
</script>
```

Model

```
public class MyModel
{
   [DateRange("StartDate", "EndDate", ErrorMessage =
                  "MyDate should be between StartDate and EndDate.")]
   public DateOnly MyDate { get; set; }
   public DateOnly StartDate { get; set; }
   public DateOnly EndDate { get; set; }
}
```

The DateRangeAttribute class defines the custom validation attribute, which checks the date range on both the server and client sides.

The GetClientValidationRules method in the DateRangeAttribute class sets up client-side validation rules, making use of the $.validator methods to create and associate the validation logic.

The <script> block includes the necessary client-side validation logic, registering a custom validation method and creating an adapter for the daterange validation rule. This ensures that client-side validation behaves as expected.

From Attributes

In ASP.NET MVC, the attributes [FromHeader], [FromForm], [FromQuery], [FromBody], [FromRoute], and [FromServices], are used to specify the source from which action method parameters should be bound data. Each of these attributes indicates a different source of data within an HTTP request or from a service. Here's an overview of each:

1. [FromHeader] Attribute:

    Used to bind data from HTTP request headers.

    For example, [FromHeader] string acceptLanguage binds data from the "Accept-Language" header.

```
public IActionResult Login([FromHeader] string acceptLanguage)
```

2. [FromForm] Attribute:

    Used to bind data from HTML form fields (typically used with POST requests).

    For example, [FromForm] string username binds data from a form field with the name "username."

```
public IActionResult Login([FromForm] string userName)
```

3. [FromQuery] Attribute:

    Used to bind data from the query string in the URL.

    For example, [FromQuery] int page binds data from a query parameter like "?page=2" in the URL.

```
public IActionResult Get([FromQuery] int page)
```

4. [FromBody] Attribute:

    Used to bind data from the HTTP request body.

    For example, [FromBody] MyModel model binds data from the request body, which is often used when working with complex data in JSON format.

```
public IActionResult Get([FromBody] string userName)
```

5. [FromRoute] Attribute:

   Used to bind data from route parameters (parts of the URL path).

   For example, [FromRoute] int id binds data from a route parameter like "/products/{id}" in the URL.

```
[HttpGet("/products/{id}")]
public IActionResult Get([FromRoute] int id)
```

6. [FromServices] Attribute:

   Used to inject services or dependencies into an action method.

   For example, [FromServices] IMyService myService injects the IMyService service into the action method.

```
public IActionResult Get([FromServices] IMyService myService)
```

If you do not use any of the data source attributes on an action method parameter the framework will still attempt to bind the parameter values, but it will rely on default conventions to determine the data source. The binding behavior will be determined by the parameter's type, the HTTP verb of the request, and the naming of parameters.

If you don't specify [FromServices], dependencies will not be injected into the parameter.

HTTP Return Types

There are several IActionResult return types that you can use in your MVC controllers to return various HTTP status codes or results

Ok(): Returns an HTTP 200 (OK) status code, indicating a successful request. It can be used when you want to indicate that the operation was successful.

NotFound(): Returns an HTTP 404 (Not Found) status code, indicating that the requested resource could not be found. This is typically used when the requested item or page doesn't exist.

BadRequest(): Returns an HTTP 400 (Bad Request) status code, indicating that the request was invalid or malformed. You can use this when the client's request doesn't meet your API's requirements.

Unauthorized(): Returns an HTTP 401 (Unauthorized) status code, indicating that the client is not authenticated to access the requested resource. This is often used in conjunction with authentication and authorization mechanisms.

92

Forbid(): Returns an HTTP 403 (Forbidden) status code, indicating that the client is authenticated but doesn't have permission to access the requested resource. This is also used in conjunction with authentication and authorization.

InternalServerError(): Returns an HTTP 500 (Internal Server Error) status code, indicating that an unexpected error occurred on the server. It's used when something goes wrong on the server-side that is not caused by the client's request.

NoContent(): Returns an HTTP 204 (No Content) status code, indicating a successful request with no additional data to return in the response body. It's often used when an action was successful, but there's no data to send back.

CreatedAtAction(): Returns an HTTP 201 (Created) status code along with a location header that specifies where the newly created resource can be found. It's used when creating a new resource and you want to inform the client where to find it.

RedirectToAction(): Returns an HTTP 302 (Found) status code and redirects the client to another action within the application. It's used when you want to direct the client to a different URL.

```
[HttpGet]
public IActionResult Login()
{
    return Ok();
}


[HttpGet]
public IActionResult Login()
{
    return Ok(View());
}
```

NonAction

Controller actions can be marked with the [NonAction] attribute to indicate that they are not intended to be accessible as public actions. This attribute is used when you have methods in your controller class that are meant for internal use and should not be exposed as part of your application's public API.

```
[NonAction]
public IActionResult MyPrivateView()
{
    return View();
```

```
}

[HttpGet]
public IActionResult Login()
{
    return PartialView("MyPrivateView");
}
```

Web API

Web API is similar to MVC but lacks the view component. It's designed to handle HTTP requests and responses for exposing data and functionality over the web.

You can create Web API project or use the same MVC project and configure it to serve as a Web API.

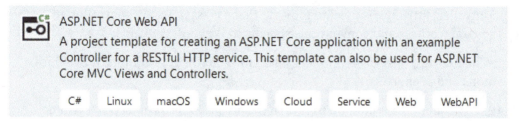

Program.cs

```
var builder = WebApplication.CreateBuilder(args);

//registering the services required for working with controllers.
builder.Services.AddControllers();

var app = builder.Build();

//maps controller actions to incoming HTTP requests.
app.MapControllers();

app.Run();
```

Controller

```
[Route("")]
[ApiController]
public class HomeController : ControllerBase
{
```

```
[HttpGet("GetDate")]
public string GetDate()
{
    return DateTime.Now.ToString();
}
}
```

The [ApiController] attribute is used to indicate that a class is an API controller. It provides several features and conventions specific to Web API controllers.

The ControllerBase is a base class for controllers in Web API applications. It provides a set of methods and properties.

In Web API controllers, it is common to return the actual value or object that will be serialized into the HTTP response directly, rather than returning an IActionResult. This approach is based on the idea of convention over configuration, where the framework handles the serialization of the returned value into the appropriate HTTP response format, typically JSON or XML.

Default HTTP Verb

In Web API, when you create an action method without specifying an HTTP verb attribute, such as [HttpGet] or [HttpPost], it will act as a default POST action. This means that if you don't explicitly specify the HTTP verb attribute, the action method will be accessible via HTTP POST requests.

```
[Route("[controller]")]
[ApiController]
public class HomeController : ControllerBase
{
    [Route("GetDate")]
    public string GetDate()
    {
        return DateTime.Now.ToString();
    }
}
```

Dependency Injection

Dependency Injection (DI) in ASP.NET is a design pattern and framework feature that enables you to manage and inject dependencies (services or objects) into your application's components, such as controllers, services, and middleware. DI promotes modularity, testability, and maintainability by decoupling components from their dependencies.

In ASP.NET, services are registered within the application's dependency injection container, which is usually provided by the built-in DI framework. You can register services in the Program.cs file.

MyService.cs

```
public class MyService
{
    public void Print() { Console.WriteLine("Hello"); }
}
```

Program.cs

```
builder.Services.AddSingleton<MyService>();
```

HomeController.cs

```
public class HomeController : Controller
{
    private MyService myService;

    public HomeController(MyService myService)
    {
        this.myService = myService;
    }

    public void MyAction()
    {
        myService.Print();
    }
}
```

MyService is a class that you want to use as a service.

builder.Services.AddSingleton<MyService>() registers MyService as a singleton service with the DI container. This means there will be a single instance of MyService shared throughout the application.

In the constructor of HomeController, we are using constructor injection to receive an instance of MyService. This is possible because you've registered MyService as a singleton in the DI container.

With interface:

Program.cs

```
builder.Services.AddSingleton<IMyService,MyService>();
```

MyService.cs

```csharp
public interface IMyService
{
    void Print();
}

public class MyService : IMyService
{
    public void Print() { Console.WriteLine("Hello"); }
}
```

```
public class HomeController : Controller
{
    private IMyService myService;


    public HomeController(IMyService myService)
    {
        this.myService = myService;
    }
}
```

Di with primary constructor

You don't have to use a constructor in dependency injection, you can utilize the primary constructor and omit the assignment in the regular constructor.

```
public class HomeController(MyService myService) : Controller
{
    public void MyAction(){ myService.Print(); }
}
```

Service Lifetimes

ASP.NET supports three main service lifetimes:

Singleton: A singleton service is created once when the application starts and is shared across all incoming requests. Its lifetime extends throughout the entire application.

Scoped: A scoped service is created once per HTTP request. It lives for the duration of that request and is disposed of at the end of the request. Scoped services are isolated to individual requests.

Transient: A transient service is created every time it is requested. It has a very short lifetime and is typically used for stateless and lightweight services.

```
builder.Services.AddSingleton<MyService>();
```

```
builder.Services.AddScoped<MyService>();
builder.Services.AddTransient<MyService>();
```

Impossible Combinations

AddSingleton inside AddScoped: This combination is not possible because a scoped service's lifetime is shorter than a singleton. A singleton service is created once and shared across the entire application, whereas a scoped service is created once per scope (usually a single HTTP request). It doesn't make sense to register a singleton service within a scoped service because the singleton will outlive the scope.

Unusual Combinations

AddTransient inside AddSingleton: This is a valid combination, but it's uncommon. It means that a new instance of the transient service will be created every time you resolve it within the singleton. Since the singleton instance is shared across the entire application, you might not need this level of granularity for a service that's intended to be shared throughout the application.

AddScoped inside AddTransient: This is also a valid combination, but it might be unusual. A new instance of the transient service will be created for each scope, and since the transient service has a shorter lifetime than the scoped service, you'll have multiple instances of the transient service per scope.

AddScoped inside AddSingleton: This is a valid combination, but it can be unusual. The scoped service is created once per scope, and the singleton is created only once and shared across the application. If you register a scoped service within a singleton, you'll effectively get a single instance of the scoped service for the entire application, which might not be what you want.

Common Combinations

AddTransient inside AddScoped: This combination is common when you want a new instance of a service for each HTTP request (scoped) and that service has a short-lived lifetime (transient).

AddScoped inside AddScoped: This is a common combination for defining services that have the same lifetime, typically within the scope of an HTTP request.

AddSingleton inside AddSingleton: This is common for defining singletons that have dependencies on other singletons.

Singleton Services and Async Methods

In .NET, a singleton service is created once and used throughout the application. All requests share the same instance of the singleton service.

Local Variables in Methods

Inside a singleton service method, local variables (defined within the method) are unique to each method call. Therefore, when handling multiple requests, each request gets its own separate instance of the method's local variables.

Async Methods and Await

Using async and await within a method allows asynchronous operations without blocking threads. The method execution pauses at await and resumes later, but each request has its own context. The await keyword does not cause data sharing between different method calls.

Concurrency and Shared State

Stateless Methods: If the service method is stateless (i.e., it does not use instance-level fields to store data), it handles multiple requests concurrently without any issues, as each request operates in isolation.

Stateful Methods: If the method uses shared state (instance fields), you must manage concurrency carefully. Without proper synchronization, multiple requests could overwrite shared data, leading to inconsistencies. To avoid this, use local variables for request-specific data or ensure that shared state is accessed in a thread-safe manner (e.g., using locks or thread-safe data structures).

Data Overwriting

Local variables within the method are not shared between requests, so data inside these variables is not overwritten. However, if a singleton service method modifies shared instance-level fields, those fields may be accessed and modified by multiple requests simultaneously, leading to potential data overwriting or race conditions.

Dependency injection (DI) with a singleton

A singleton service means that a single instance of the service is created for the lifetime of the application.

Every time the service is injected (regardless of the scope), all consumers receive the same instance.

Handling Multiple Requests

When you have a singleton service handling 1000 requests, the same service instance will be used across all requests. If the service has internal state (like fields or properties), all requests share that state.

However, if you're using await within your singleton service methods, here's how it works. When you use await inside a method, it does not block the thread. The method's execution is paused until the awaited task completes, then it resumes. The execution context is captured and restored when the await completes.

If your singleton service is stateless (i.e., it doesn't store any data in fields or properties between method calls), you don't need to worry about concurrency issues.

If the service is stateful (i.e., it holds data in fields or properties), multiple requests may read and write the same data concurrently. This can lead to race conditions where data is overwritten or inconsistent. You can mitigate this by using thread synchronization mechanisms like lock, or by using thread-safe data structures.

Preventing Overwrites in Async Methods

If your singleton holds state, you need to make sure that two requests don't overwrite the same data at the same time. Here are some strategies:

Avoid Shared State: Keep your singleton stateless by avoiding fields or properties that store per-request data. Instead, pass data through method parameters.

Thread Safety: If you must store shared state, ensure access to it is thread-safe. For example, you can use the lock keyword to ensure only one request can modify the data at a time:

Use Local Variables: If you're working with asynchronous operations, ensure that each request operates on its own local data (local variables within methods), which won't interfere with other requests.

Scoped or Transient Services for Per-Request State: If you need per-request data but don't want shared state, consider using scoped or transient services for parts of your logic.

Conclusion

If your singleton service is stateless, you can handle thousands of requests without any issues.

If your singleton service is stateful, you must manage concurrency carefully to prevent race conditions and data overwrites. You can do this by avoiding shared state, making your code thread-safe, or using scoped/transient services for request-specific data.

When you have a singleton service in .NET and handle multiple requests using async and await, if you wonder how data inside the method is not overwritten. Let's break down how this works.

Local Variables in Methods: Local variables (inside the function) are unique to each call of the method. So, when your service method is invoked multiple times (even simultaneously), each invocation has its own separate "copy" of the local variables.

State within Awaited Calls: The await keyword does not cause data to be shared between different method invocations. The execution of the method pauses when it hits await, but when the awaited task completes, the method resumes where it left off. Each invocation of the method has its own context, including its own local variables, which prevents data overwriting.

Concurrency: As long as you avoid sharing state between requests (i.e., not using instance-level fields), each request will execute its own copy of the method, and local data within the method won't interfere with other requests.

Example

Let's take a simple example where you have a singleton service and a method that handles asynchronous operations:

```csharp
public class MySingletonService
{
    public async Task<string> DoWorkAsync(string requestId)
    {
        // Local variables are unique to each request
        string result = $"Processing request {requestId}";

        // Simulate asynchronous work
        await Task.Delay(1000);
```

```
      // Local variables are not shared between requests
      result += $" - Completed request {requestId}";
      return result;

  }

}
```

What Happens When Multiple Requests Hit This Method?

Local Variables Are Isolated: The variable result is a local variable inside the DoWorkAsync method. Each request that calls this method will have its own version of the result variable. This means that the data inside the function is not shared across requests.

Async Execution: When the method hits await Task.Delay(1000);, the method is paused until the task completes. While it's paused, other requests can still invoke the method. Each invocation will have its own context and its own copy of the result variable.

No Data Overwriting: Since each method call has its own local variables, there is no overwriting between requests. Each request operates in isolation, even if the service is a singleton.

If you send multiple requests, like this:

```
await service.DoWorkAsync("Request1");

await service.DoWorkAsync("Request2");
```

The first request will have its own copy of the local variables (like result), and the second request will have its own, separate copy.

Even if both requests are being processed at the same time, their local state remains isolated, and data from one request won't affect the other.

When Does Overwriting Occur?

Overwriting occurs only If you use fields in your singleton class (outside the method) to store data, multiple requests will share that data, potentially leading to overwrites.

For example:

```
public class MySingletonService

{

    private string sharedState;  // This is shared by all requests
```

```csharp
public async Task<string> DoWorkAsync(string requestId)
{

    // This can lead to overwriting
    sharedState = $"Processing request {requestId}";


    await Task.Delay(1000);


    sharedState += $" - Completed request {requestId}";
    return sharedState;  // This can return an inconsistent result

}
}
```

In this case, sharedState is shared between requests, so one request could overwrite the data of another request. To avoid this, keep state local within methods, or use thread-safe mechanisms.

Summary:

Local variables inside async methods are isolated per invocation and won't be overwritten by other requests.

Await doesn't cause issues, as it just pauses the method and resumes it later with its own state.

Avoid instance fields in singleton services if the data needs to remain unique per request.

This design ensures that data inside your function (local variables) is not overwritten when handling multiple requests.

RequestServices

It provides access to the service provider associated with the current HTTP request. This property allows you to resolve services within the scope of the current request.

GetService

GetService is a method that allows you to access the service provider and retrieve a service instance within the scope of an HTTP request.

```
public class HomeController : Controller
{
    public void MyAction()
    {
      var myService = HttpContext
              .RequestServices
              .GetService<MyService>();

    }
}
```

If MyService is not registered, it will return null.

GetRequiredService

GetRequiredService is similar to RequiredService except if the service is not registered, GetRequiredService will throw an exception indicating the service couldn't be resolved.

```
var myService = HttpContext
        .RequestServices
        .GetRequiredService<MyService>();
```

Middleware

Middleware are modules that are added to the application's request pipeline to handle HTTP requests and responses, allowing you to build and customize the behavior of your application.

Request Pipeline

Middleware modules are organized in a request pipeline. Each incoming HTTP request flows through the pipeline, and middleware modules can inspect, modify, or generate responses based on the request.

Order of Execution

Middleware components are executed in the order they are added to the pipeline. This allows you to control the order of processing and implement various features, such as authentication, routing, logging, and error handling.

Built-In Middleware

ASP.NET provides a range of built-in middleware components for common tasks, such as authentication, authorization, routing, caching, and compression. You can use these components or create custom middleware to suit your application's needs.

Custom Middleware

You can create custom middleware components to add application-specific behavior. Custom middleware is written as C# classes with specific methods for handling requests and responses. For example, you can create middleware for logging, authentication, or other application-specific tasks.

Middleware Terminators

Some middleware modules can terminate the request pipeline, such as authentication middleware. These components may either continue processing or return a response directly, bypassing subsequent middleware.

Error Handling

Middleware components can also handle exceptions and errors that occur during request processing, providing customized error responses or logging.

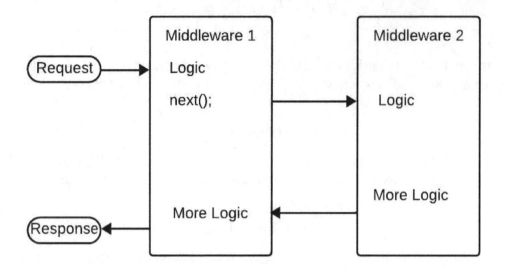

The order in which you add middleware in your application is crucial, as it determines the sequence in which the middleware components handle incoming requests and outgoing responses.

Error middleware

A simple custom middleware to handle all uncaught errors in the application. This middleware captures exceptions that occur during the processing of HTTP requests and logs them.

```csharp
public class ErrorMiddleware
{
    private readonly RequestDelegate next;

    public ErrorMiddleware(RequestDelegate next)
    {
        this.next = next;
    }

    public async Task InvokeAsync(HttpContext context)
    {
        try
        {
            await next(context);
        }
        catch (Exception ex){ // log error in database }
    }
}
```

The constructor of the ErrorMiddleware class takes an instance of RequestDelegate as a parameter. The RequestDelegate represents the next middleware component in the pipeline. It allows the middleware to pass the request to the next middleware component after processing.

The InvokeAsync method is the entry point for the middleware's logic. When an HTTP request is received, this method is called.

Inside the InvokeAsync method, the code is wrapped in a try-catch block. It attempts to invoke the next middleware in the pipeline by calling await next(context).

If an exception is thrown during the execution of the next middleware or any subsequent middleware in the pipeline, the catch block captures the exception (stored in the ex variable). You can then add error handling or logging logic to this block to respond to the exception.

Register the Middleware in the Program.cs file to the request pipeline.

```
app.UseMiddleware<ErrorMiddleware>();
```

Filters

Filter pipeline is similar to middleware pipeline in many ways, but they also have some differences that should be considered when deciding which approach to be used.

Similarities

Request and Response Flow: Both middleware and filters are components that can process incoming requests and outgoing responses. They are part of the request and response flow in an ASP.NET application.

Short-Circuiting: Both middleware and filters can short-circuit the request/response pipeline by directly returning a response. This allows them to stop further processing and return a response immediately.

Cross-Cutting Concerns: Both middleware and filters are used to handle cross-cutting concerns in web applications, such as logging, performance profiling, or exception handling.

Differences

Scope of Execution:

Middleware: Middleware can run for all requests that pass through the middleware pipeline. They are not limited to specific controllers or actions.

Filters: Filters are typically applied to a subset of requests, such as a specific controller or action. They provide a more granular way to apply behavior.

Access to MVC Components:

Middleware: Middleware operates at a lower level and is independent of MVC or Razor Pages. They don't have direct access to MVC components like ModelState or IActionResults.

Filters: Filters have access to MVC components and can interact with them. They are designed to work with MVC-specific features.

Design for Specific Requests:

Middleware: Middleware is not designed to be applied to a specific set of requests. It operates globally for all requests that pass through the pipeline.

Filters: Filters are designed to be applied selectively to specific controllers, actions, or pages. They allow you to target specific parts of the application.

Custom validation filter

```csharp
public class ModelStateValidationFilter : IAsyncActionFilter
{
  public async Task OnActionExecutionAsync(ActionExecutingContext context,
                          ActionExecutionDelegate next)
  {
    if (!context.ModelState.IsValid)
    {
      context.Result = new JsonResult(new
      {
        IsError = true, Errors = GetErrors(context.ModelState)
      });
    }
    else
    {
      await next();
    }
  }

  public string GetErrors(ModelStateDictionary modelState)
  {
    StringBuilder errors = new StringBuilder();
    for (int i = 0; i < modelState.Count; i++)
    {
      var err = modelState?.Values.ElementAt(i)?.Errors?.FirstOrDefault();
      if (string.IsNullOrEmpty(err?.ErrorMessage))
      {
        errors.Append($"{modelState?.ElementAt(i).Key} is Invalid. ");
      }
      else
      {
        errors.Append($"{err?.ErrorMessage} ");
      }
    }
    return errors.ToString();
  }
}
```

```
}
```

Implementation of an action filter. It's designed to handle model state validation, and if the model state is not valid, it returns a JSON result containing error information.

Th ModelStateValidationFilter class implements the IAsyncActionFilter interface, which allows it to be applied as an action filter. It contains an OnActionExecutionAsync method that is invoked before and after the execution of an action. It checks if the ModelState is not valid. If the model state is invalid, it constructs a JSON result with error information and sets it as the result of the action. If the model state is valid, it proceeds to execute the action by calling await next().

GetErrors(): Used to generate error messages based on the ModelState object.

It iterates through the model state, checks for errors, and constructs an error message if any are found.

If you want to redirect to an error page instead of returning JSON, then use:

```
context.Result = new RedirectToActionResult(
"Error",
"HomeController",
GetErrors(context.ModelState));
```

Another option:

```
context.Result = new RedirectResult("/Error");
```

Finally, to use the ModelStateValidationFilter in your app, you need to add it to the program.cs file.

Use the filter globally

```
builder.Services.AddControllersWithViews(x =>
{
    x.Filters.Add<ModelStateValidationFilter>();
});
```

ASP.NET have default response when the ModelState is invalid:

```
{
  "type": "https://tools.ietf.org/html/rfc9110#section-15.5.1",
  "title": "One or more validation errors occurred.",
  "status": 400,
  "errors": {
    "email": [ "The email field is required." ],
    "password": [ "The password field is required." ]
  },
  "traceId": "00-3a3b87c614543f40be96dd49905032ee-baf7784a8a5e1b5d-00"
}
```

So, to disabled it you need to add this:

```
services.AddControllers()
.ConfigureApiBehaviorOptions(options =>
{
    options.SuppressModelStateInvalidFilter = true;
});
```

This option allows you to suppress the default behavior of automatically returning a 400 Bad Request response when model state validation fails.

The reason for suppressing the default behavior is to maintain a uniform response structure across the API.

Use the filter on specific action

You don't have to use your filter on all controllers, you can use it only on a specific controller or action if you inherit the Attribute class.

```
class ModelStateValidationFilter : Attribute, IAsyncActionFilter
```

```
[ModelStateValidationFilter]
[HttpPost]
public IActionResult Login(LoginModel login)
```

Or you can use the TypeFilter Attribute:

```
[TypeFilter(typeof(ModelStateValidationFilter))]
[HttpPost]
public IActionResult Login(LoginModel login)
```

Or you can use the ServiceFilter Attribute:

```
[ServiceFilter(typeof(ModelStateValidationFilter))]
[HttpPost]
public IActionResult Login(LoginModel login)
```

but when using service filter, you must add the ModelStateValidationFilter to the di:

```
services.AddSingleton<ModelStateValidationFilter>();
```

Types of Filters

In ASP.NET, there are several types of filters that can be used to perform various actions or execute code at different stages of the request and response pipeline.

This diagram illustrates the sequential execution of filter types within the MVC filter pipeline. Each filter type plays a specific role in enhancing the application's behavior and functionality.

While it may seem like there are many filters, each type of filter serves a distinct purpose, and you may not need to use all of them in every application. The reason for having multiple filters is to provide flexibility and separation of concerns in your application.

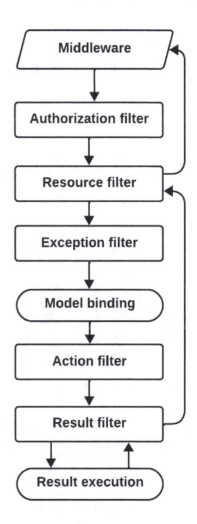

Authorization Filters:

- Execution Order: First
- Purpose: Determine user authorization for the requested resource
- Action: Short-circuit the pipeline if authorization fails

Resource Filters:

- Execution Order: After Authorization Filters
- Purpose: Perform operations on the request or response

Action Filters:

- Execution Order: Before and After the Action Method
- Purpose: Modify action method arguments or return values
- Note: Not supported in Razor Pages

Endpoint Filters:

- Execution Order: Before and After the Action Method
- Purpose: Modify action method arguments or return values
- Note: Not supported in Razor Pages
- Applicable: Actions and route handler-based endpoints

Exception Filters:

- Execution Order: Handle unhandled exceptions before the response body is written
- Purpose: Apply global policies to unhandled exceptions

Authorization Filters

These filters are used to enforce authorization rules, and they run early in the request pipeline. They are responsible for determining if a user is allowed to access a particular resource. The [Authorize] attribute is a commonly used authorization filter.

```csharp
public class MyAuthorizationFilter : IAsyncAuthorizationFilter
{
    public async Task OnAuthorizationAsync(AuthorizationFilterContext context)
    {
        if (await IsUserAuthorized())
        {
            context.Result = new ForbidResult();
            return;
        }
    }

    private async Task<bool> IsUserAuthorized()
    {
        // authorization logic
        // For example, check user access in a database
        return true;
    }
}
```

Action Filters

Action Filters allow you to execute code before or after the execution of an action method in a controller. An example of the action filter shown above in the custom validation filter.

Resource Filters

Resource filters run just before the MVC action is executed and are used to manipulate the result of an action.

They allow you to perform operations on the result returned by the action method.

```csharp
public class ModelStateValidationFilter : IAsyncResourceFilter
```

```csharp
{
    public async Task OnResourceExecutionAsync(
                ResourceExecutingContext context,
                ResourceExecutionDelegate next)
    {
        var ipAddress = context.HttpContext.Connection.RemoteIpAddress;
        await next();
    }
}
```

Exception Filters

Exception filters are used to handle exceptions that occur during the execution of an action. They provide a way to customize how exceptions are handled, logged, or presented to the user.

```
public class ModelStateValidationFilter : IAsyncExceptionFilter
{
    public async Task OnExceptionAsync(ExceptionContext context)
    {
        //Log the exception or perform other error handling tasks


        //create a response
        context.Result = new ObjectResult("An error occurred")
        {
            StatusCode = StatusCodes.Status500InternalServerError
        };
    }
}
```

Result Filters

Result filters are applied after an action method has completed and a result has been produced. They allow you to modify the result, perform logging, or other post-processing tasks.

```
public class ModelStateValidationFilter : IAsyncResultFilter
{
    public async Task OnResultExecutionAsync(
                ResultExecutingContext context,
                ResultExecutionDelegate next)
    {
        var request = context.HttpContext.Request;
        if (request.Headers.Any(x=> x.Key == "hi-Header"))
        {
            var response = context.HttpContext.Response;
            response.Headers.Add("bye-header","true");
        }
    }
}
```

}

Caching

Caching is a mechanism used to store and retrieve frequently used data in a faster and more efficient manner. It works by temporarily storing copies of data in a location that allows for quick access, reducing the need to repeatedly fetch or compute the same data from its original source.

MemoryCache

ASP.NET includes a built-in in-memory caching provider called MemoryCache. You can use it to store data in memory within your application.

```csharp
public class HomeController : Controller
{
    private IMemoryCache memoryCache;

    public HomeController(IMemoryCache memoryCache)
    {
        this.memoryCache = memoryCache;
    }

    [HttpGet]
    public List<Product> GetProducts()
    {
        // get products from cache
        var products = memoryCache.Get("products") as List<Product>;
        if (products is null)
        {
            // get products from db
            List<Product> dbProducts = new();

            // save products in cache
            memoryCache.Set("products", dbProducts);

            return dbProducts;
        }
        return products;
    }
```

```
}
```

```
builder.Services.AddSingleton<IMemoryCache, MemoryCache>();
```

In GetProducts action method, we attempt to retrieve a list of products from the cache by using the memoryCache.Get method. We provide a key, in this case,

In the GetProducts action method, we attempt to retrieve a list of products from the cache using the memoryCache.Get method. We provide a key, in this case, "products," to identify the data we wish to retrieve. If the products are found in the cache (a cache hit), we return the cached list of products. If the products are not found in the cache (a cache miss), we retrieve the products from the database (stored in dbProducts) and then store this list in the cache using the memoryCache.Set method. This allows subsequent requests to efficiently retrieve the data from the cache, as accessing data from memory is faster than from the database.

Be careful: When you store an object in IMemoryCache, you are storing a reference to that object. Consequently, if you modify the object after it has been cached, those changes will also be reflected in the cached version because both the cached object and the original object refer to the same instance.

Expiration

In MemoryCache, you can set an expiration time for cached items to determine when an item is considered expired and should be removed from the cache.

```
List<Product> dbProducts = new();
memoryCache.Set("products",dbProducts,TimeSpan.FromMinutes(30));
```

It stores the dbProducts list with the key "products" and specifies that the cached items will expire after 30 minutes. After 30 minutes, if you attempt to access the data with the key "products," it will result in a cache miss.

Sliding Expiration: Sliding expiration allows you to set a time duration, and the expiration timer is reset every time the item is accessed. If the item is not accessed within the specified time duration, it will expire and be removed from the cache.

```
List <Product> dbProducts = new();
var options = new MemoryCacheEntryOptions
{
    SlidingExpiration = TimeSpan.FromMinutes(30)
};
```

```
memoryCache.Set("products", dbProducts, options);
```

OutputCache

OutputCache is an attribute that allows you to cache the output of controller actions or entire views, which can significantly improve the performance of your application by reducing the need to regenerate the same content repeatedly.

Program.cs

```
builder.Services.AddOutputCache();
app.UseOutputCache();
```

Cache an Action

```
[OutputCache(Duration = 60)]
public List<Product> GetProducts()
```

The [OutputCache] attribute specifies that the output of that action should be cached for a duration of 60 seconds. When a user makes a request to the action, the output generated by the action (e.g., the HTML view or content) will be cached for a period of 60 seconds. During this 60-second duration, if other users access the same action, they will receive the cached output without the action being executed again. This can significantly reduce the server load and improve response times, especially for actions that generate static or rarely changing content. After the 60-second duration elapses, the cache is considered stale, and the next request to the action will execute the action method to generate fresh output, which is then cached for another 60 seconds.

VaryByQueryKeys

VaryByQueryKeys property is used within the [ResponseCache] attribute to control caching behavior based on specific query string parameters. It allows you to specify which query string parameters should be considered when determining whether to serve a cached response or generate a fresh one.

```
[OutputCache(Duration = 60, VaryByQueryKeys = new[]{" id" } )]
[HttpGet]
public List<Product> GetProducts()
```

The [OutputCache] attribute specifies that the response from the GetProducts action should be cached for 60 seconds and should vary based on the "id" query parameter. If the "id" query parameter changes, it will trigger a new cache entry for that specific "id" value.

https://localhost:7223/GetProducts/?id=1 - The response for this URL with id=1 will be cached.

https://localhost:7223/GetProducts/?id=1 (a repeat of the first URL) - This request will retrieve the cached response based on the id=1 query parameter.

https://localhost:7223/GetProducts/?id=2 - This URL has a different id parameter (id=2). The response for this URL will be cached separately from the others and will vary based on the id=2 query parameter.

You can also use VaryByHeaderNames and VaryByRouteValueNames within the [OutputCache] attribute to control caching behavior based on HTTP headers and route values, respectively.

ResponseCache

ResponseCache is similar to OutputCache, but it has the ability to control caching in the browser, with the ResponseCacheLocation enum.

```
public enum ResponseCacheLocation
{
    //Cached in both proxies/server and client, default value.
    //Sets "Cache-control" header to "public".
    Any = 0,
    //Cached only in the client.
    //Sets "Cache-control" header to "private".
    Client = 1,
    //"Cache-control" and "Pragma" headers are set to "no-cache".
    None = 2
}
```

```
[ResponseCache(Duration = 60,
        Location = ResponseCacheLocation.Client)]
[HttpGet]
public List<Product> GetProducts()
```

Program.cs

```
builder.Services.AddResponseCaching();
app.UseResponseCaching();
```

When using ResponseCache, the server returns a 'Cache-Control' header to the browser with the 'max-age' directive: 'Cache-Control: public, max-age=60'. The browser is responsible for caching the values on the client side.

For UI applications such as Razor Pages, the ResponseCache attribute might not be as beneficial. This is because web browsers often set request headers that prevent caching of UI-related requests. For UI apps, output caching might be more suitable, as it allows configuration-based control over what should be cached independently of HTTP headers.

Cache Tag Helper

The Cache Tag Helper allows you to cache portions of your Razor views. It's useful for optimizing the performance of your web application by caching the rendering of specific content fragments, such as partial views or components.

```
<cache expires-after="@TimeSpan.FromMinutes(30)"
vary-by-query="id">
  Hi
</cache>
```

Configuration

Configuration is an aspect of the application setup. It allows you to externalize settings from your code, making your application more flexible and easier to manage across different environments.

launchSettings.json

The launchSettings.json is a configuration file used primarily during development. It specifies how your application will be launched and debugged in various environments, such as IIS Express, Kestrel, Docker, etc. This file is typically found under the Properties folder of your project.

launchSettings.json

```json
{
  "iisSettings": {
    "windowsAuthentication": false,
    "anonymousAuthentication": true,
    "iisExpress": {
      "applicationUrl": "http://localhost:5005",
      "sslPort": 44305
    }
  },
  "profiles": {
    "MyApp": {
      "commandName": "Project",
      "dotnetRunMessages": "true",
      "launchBrowser": true,
      "environmentVariables": {
        "ASPNETCORE_ENVIRONMENT": "Development"
      },
      "applicationUrl":
          "https://localhost:5001;http://localhost:5000"
    }
  }
}
```

Under the "iisSettings" key, you can configure settings related to IIS Express if you're using Windows.

Under the "profiles" key, you define different profiles for launching your application.

"MyApp" is an example profile name.

"commandName" specifies how the application should be launched. "Project" means the project will be run directly using dotnet run.

"dotnetRunMessages" controls whether dotnet run command messages are displayed.

"launchBrowser" determines whether a browser should be opened when the application starts.

"environmentVariables" allows you to specify environment variables. Here, we set ASPNETCORE_ENVIRONMENT to "Development".

"applicationUrl" specifies the URLs where your application will be hosted.

You can add additional profiles as needed for different environments (e.g., Staging, Production) or for different launch configurations.

IConfiguration

The IConfiguration interface used to retrieve data from Configuration files. JSON files are commonly used for storing configuration data. By default, ASP.NET looks for appsettings.json. You can create custom configuration providers to read configuration data from other sources such as databases, XML files, or any other external storage.

Create these extensions for easier use:

```csharp
public static class ConfigExtensions
{
    public static T Get<T>(this IConfiguration conf,
                                string key)
    {
        return conf.GetSection(key).Get<T>();
    }
    public static string Get(this IConfiguration conf,
                                string key)
    {
        return conf.GetSection(key).Value;
    }
}
```

appsettings.json

```json
{
  "password": "1234", "age": 30
}
```

```csharp
[ApiController][Route("")]
public class MyController(IConfiguration conf) : Controller
{
  [HttpGet("configuration")]
  public void Configuration()
  {
     var password = conf.Get<string>("password");
     var age = conf.Get<byte>("age");
  }

}
```

The IConfiguration parameter will be injected by the ASP.NET Core DI container.

Within the Configuration() action method, GetValue<T>() method of the IConfiguration interface is used to retrieve configuration values. Here, we retrieve the values of "Password" and "Age" configuration keys and cast them to the appropriate types (string and byte respectively).

Add configuration files

```
// Additional JSON configuration file
builder.Configuration.AddJsonFile(Path.Combine(AppContext.BaseDirectory,
"additionalsettings.json"),  optional: true, reloadOnChange: true);
```

builder.Configuration provides access to the application's configuration.

.AddJsonFile() is used to add JSON configuration files directly to the configuration builder instance.

optional: true, indicate that appsettings.json is required.

reloadOnChange: true, indicate that should be reloaded if changed.

additionalsettings.json

```
{
  "date": "01-01-2000"
}
```

```
var date = conf.Get<string>("date");
```

Different environments

You can create separate appsettings.json files for different environments by following a naming convention. ASP.NET automatically selects the appropriate configuration file based on the environment in which the application is running.

appsettings.json: This is the default configuration file that contains settings common to all environments.

appsettings.Development.json: This file contains settings specific to the development environment. It overrides settings from the appsettings.json file when the application is running in the development environment.

appsettings.Production.json: This file contains settings specific to the production environment. It overrides settings from the appsettings.json file when the application is running in the production environment.

You can also create environment-specific JSON files for other environments as needed (e.g., appsettings.Staging.json).

Add the ASPNETCORE_ENVIRONMENT variable for each profile in your launchSettings.json, you would add it within the environmentVariables property of each profile.

launchSettings.json

```
"profiles": {
 "Development": {
  "environmentVariables": {
   "ASPNETCORE_ENVIRONMENT": "Development"
  }
 },
 "Staging": {
  "environmentVariables": {
   "ASPNETCORE_ENVIRONMENT": "Staging"
  }
 },
 "Production": {
  "environmentVariables": {
   "ASPNETCORE_ENVIRONMENT": "Production"
  }
 }
}
```

Static files / wwwroot folder

The wwwroot folder is a convention used in web development, particularly in ASP.NET and other web frameworks. It's a special folder where you place static files (such as HTML, CSS, JavaScript, images, etc.) that you want to serve to clients over HTTP.

Location: the wwwroot folder is located at the root level of your web project. It's automatically recognized by the framework.

Static Files: Any files placed within the wwwroot folder are considered static files. These files are served directly to clients by the web server without any processing by the application code.

Serving Files: When a client requests a file from your web application (e.g., http://site.com/css/style.css), the server looks for the file in the wwwroot folder and serves it if found.

Security: The contents of the wwwroot folder are publicly accessible by default. Ensure that you don't place sensitive files in this folder unless they're intended to be served to clients.

Usage: You can organize files within the wwwroot folder in any way that makes sense for your application's structure. For example, you might have subfolders for CSS, JavaScript, images, fonts, etc.

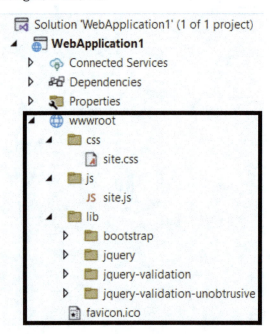

To serve static files, you need to add the Static Files Middleware to your application's request processing pipeline.

Program.cs

```
app.UseStaticFiles();
```

Serving files outside of the wwwroot folder

Serving files outside of the wwwroot folder, or serving files from arbitrary locations on the file system, requires additional configuration. You can achieve this using the UseStaticFiles middleware along with some additional options.

Set up a custom file provider: You need to create a custom IFileProvider implementation that points to the directory where your files are located.

Configure the Static Files Middleware to use the custom file provider.

Program.cs

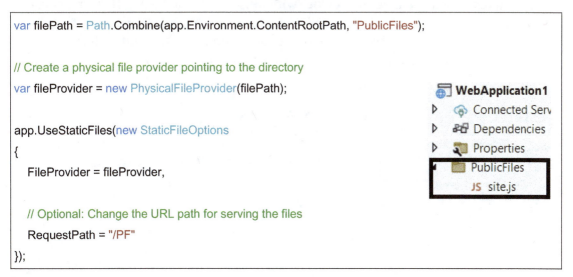

```
var filePath = Path.Combine(app.Environment.ContentRootPath, "PublicFiles");

// Create a physical file provider pointing to the directory
var fileProvider = new PhysicalFileProvider(filePath);

app.UseStaticFiles(new StaticFileOptions
{
    FileProvider = fileProvider,

    // Optional: Change the URL path for serving the files
    RequestPath = "/PF"
});
```

To access files, use the url:

https://localhost:7255/pf/site.js

Cookie

Cookies are small pieces of data that websites store on the user device to remember information about the user or their preferences. They are typically used to enhance the user experience by allowing websites to remember actions or preferences across different pages or visits.

Setting a cookie

```
[HttpGet("addCookie")]
public void AddCookie()
{
    Response.Cookies.Append("MyCookie", "Eldar");
}
```

This line adds a cookie named "MyCookie" with the value "Eldar" to the HTTP response. Response refers to the HttpResponse object associated with the current request. The Cookies property provides access to the collection of cookies associated with the response. The Append method is used to add a new cookie to this collection.

Press F12 to open chrome developer tools:

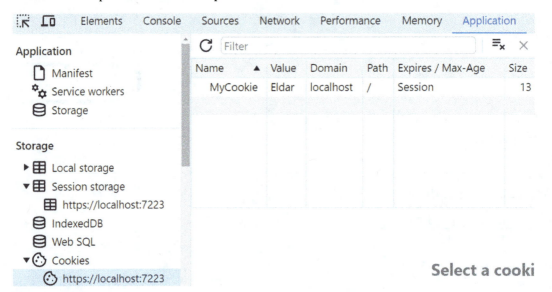

You should now see a list of cookies set by the current website. Look for a cookie named "MyCookie" with the value "Eldar" if the code provided earlier was executed successfully.

Options for Cookie

When setting a cookie, you can specify various options such as expiration time.

```
var options = new CookieOptions
{
    Expires = DateTime.Now.AddDays(1)
};
Response.Cookies.Append("MyCookie", "Eldar", options);
```

This sets the Expires property of the CookieOptions object, specifying the expiration date and time for the cookie. In this case, it's set to one day (24 hours) from the current date and time. After this time, the cookie will be removed from the browser.

More options

Domain: Specifies the domain to which the cookie applies. The cookie will be sent with requests to this domain and its subdomains. Default values is "/".

Path: Specifies the URL path to which the cookie applies. The cookie will only be sent with requests that match this path or its subpaths. For instance, setting Path to "/subfolder" would make the cookie available only to requests within the "/subfolder" path.

Secure: Whether the cookie should only be sent over HTTPS connections.

SameSite: Specifies the SameSite attribute of the cookie, which controls when the browser sends the cookie with cross-origin requests. Values are SameSiteMode.Strict, SameSiteMode.Lax, SameSiteMode.None, or SameSiteMode.Unspecified.

HttpOnly: When set to true, this property indicates that the cookie should only be accessible through HTTP requests and cannot be accessed via client-side scripts such as JavaScript. This is a security measure to mitigate certain types of cross-site scripting (XSS) attacks.

MaxAge: Specifies the maximum age of the cookie in seconds. Similar to Expires, but MaxAge specifies the maximum age relative to the time the cookie is set, rather than an absolute date and time.

IsEssential: Indicates whether the cookie is essential for the operation of the application. Essential cookies are exempt from the SameSite attribute requirements when using cross-site cookies with third-party contexts.

Get a cookie

When a web browser makes an HTTP request to a server, it includes any relevant cookies that have been previously set for the domain and path of the requested resource. These cookies are sent as part of the request headers.

The server, upon receiving the request, can then read these cookies from the request headers to access information stored in them.

```
var cookieValue = Request.Cookies["MyCookie"];
```

The variable cookieValue will contain the value of the "MyCookie" cookie if it exists in the incoming request, or it will be null if the cookie is not present.

Delete a cookie

This line of code deletes the cookie named "MyCookie" from the HTTP response. When the browser receives this response, it will remove the specified cookie from its storage.

```
Response.Cookies.Delete("MyCookie");
```

Session

A session is a collection of data stored in the server's memory that keeps track of information related to users.

A session is commonly used after a user logs in to a website. It helps store basic user data like their role, indicating if the user is logged in or not. This stored information allows the website to quickly determine if the user has access to certain pages without needing to repeatedly check the database, thus improving the server's performance.

Let's create these extension methods for easier use with types in sessions:

```
public static class SessionExtensions
{
  public static void Set<T>(this ISession session, string key, T value)
  {
    session.SetString(key, JsonSerializer.Serialize(value));
  }


  public static T Get<T>(this ISession session, string key)
  {
    var value = session.GetString(key);
    JsonSerializerOptions op = new()
    {
      PropertyNameCaseInsensitive = true,
      Converters = { new JsonStringEnumConverter() }
    };
    return value == null ? default : JsonSerializer.Deserialize<T>(value, op);
  }
}
```

The ISession interface represents a user session and provides a way to store and retrieve session data.

Program.cs

```
// add the AddSession method to enable session support.
builder.Services.AddSession();


// add the UseSession middleware to the request pipeline.
app.UseSession();
```

Set session

```
[HttpGet("login")]
public void Login(string email, string password)
{
    User user = GetUserFromDB(email, password);
    HttpContext.Session.Set("UserContext", user);
```

142

```
}
```

```
private User GetUserFromDB(string email, string password)
{
    return new User() { UserId = "1", Role = Role.Admin };
}

public enum Role {Admin = 1, User = 2 }

public class User
{
  public string UserId { get; set; }
  public Role Role { get; set; }
}
```

This is an action method responsible for handling the login request. It takes email and password parameters as input.

User user = GetUserFromDB(email, password): This line calls the GetUserFromDB method to retrieve user information from the database based on the provided email and password. In the provided code, it returns a mock User object with a UserId of "1" and a Role of "Admin".

HttpContext.Session.Set("UserContext", user): This line stores the retrieved User object in the session with the key "UserContext". It utilizes the Set extension method from the SessionExtensions class to serialize the User object and store it in the session.

Get session

```
[HttpGet("admin")]
public IActionResult Admin()
{
  var user = HttpContext.Session.Get<User>("UserContext");
  if(user != null && user.Role == Role.Admin)
  {
    return View("~/Views/AdminPage");
  }
  return View("~/Views/UnauthorizedPage");
}
```

This is the action method responsible for handling requests to the admin page.

var user = HttpContext.Session.Get<User>("UserContext"): This line retrieves the user object stored in the session with the key "UserContext" using the Get extension method provided by your SessionExtensions class. It assumes that the User class represents user information, and the session key "UserContext" was previously set during the user's login process.

if(user != null && user.Role == Role.Admin): This condition checks if the user object exists in the session and if the user has the "Admin" role. If both conditions are true, the user is considered authenticated as an admin.

return View("~/Views/AdminPage"): If the user is authenticated as an admin, this line returns the "AdminPage" view.

return View("~/Views/UnauthorizedPage"): If the user is not authenticated or does not have the admin role, this line returns the "UnauthorizedPage" view.

Overall, this code snippet demonstrates an authorization mechanism in where access to the admin page is restricted to users with the admin role. If the user is not authenticated or does not have the admin role, they are redirected to an unauthorized page.

Remove session

The provided logout endpoint handles the removes of the user context from the session, effectively logging the user out.

```
[HttpGet("logout")]
public void Logout()
{
    HttpContext.Session.Remove("UserContext");
}
```

SessionOptions

```
builder.Services.AddSession(options =>
{
    options.Cookie.Name = "cookie_name";
    options.Cookie.Path = "/";
    options.Cookie.Domain = "/";
    options.Cookie.SecurePolicy = CookieSecurePolicy.None;
    options.Cookie.SameSite = SameSiteMode.Strict;
    options.IdleTimeout = TimeSpan.FromMinutes(30);
    options.IOTimeout = TimeSpan.FromMinutes(30);
    options.Cookie.MaxAge = TimeSpan.FromMinutes(30);
    options.Cookie.HttpOnly = true;
    options.Cookie.IsEssential = true;
});
```

Name: Sets the name of the session cookie to "cookie_name". The session cookie is a small piece of data stored in the client's browser to identify the user's session.

Path: Sets the path of the session cookie to "/". The cookie will be sent with requests to any path within the domain.

Domain: Sets the domain of the session cookie to "/". The cookie will be sent with requests to any subdomain within the same domain.

SecurePolicy: Sets the HTTPS enforcement policy for the session cookie to None, meaning the cookie can be sent over both secure (HTTPS) and non-secure (HTTP) connections.

SameSite: Sets the SameSite attribute of the session cookie to Strict. The cookie will only be sent with "same-site" requests, providing protection against cross-site request forgery (CSRF) attacks.

IdleTimeout: Sets the duration of inactivity (no requests) after which a session is considered expired to 30 minutes. If the user is inactive for 30 minutes, their session will expire.

IOTimeout: Sets the maximum duration for I/O operations related to session data storage to 30 minutes. It helps prevent long-running I/O operations from blocking the request pipeline.

MaxAge: Sets the maximum age of the session cookie to 30 minutes. After this duration, the session cookie will expire on the client's browser.

HttpOnly: Sets the HttpOnly attribute of the session cookie to true, ensuring that the cookie is only accessible through HTTP requests and not through client-side scripts like JavaScript.

IsEssential: Marks the session cookie as essential for the application. It indicates that the cookie is necessary for the application's core functionality.

Session Identification

Session identification is the process of uniquely identifying each session to differentiate it from others. This identification is often achieved through the use of session cookies. When a user initiates a session, the server generates a unique identifier (session ID) and associates it with the user's interactions during that session. This session ID is then passed back and forth between the client (e.g., web browser) and server to maintain the session state.

Cookie in chrome that contains long string that represents the session id:

Name		Value	Domain	Path	Expires / Max-Age	Size
.AspNetCore.Session	▲	CfDJ8BFSUdujrglBk4lTOiCnvJM3nrG...	localhost	/	Session	203

Session lifetime

Session lifetime refers to the duration for which a session remains active. It is typically defined by a timeout period, after which the session is considered expired and no longer valid. Session times can vary depending on the application's requirements and security considerations. For example, a banking application might have shorter session times for security reasons, while a casual gaming website might have longer session times to accommodate extended periods of gameplay.

Automatic session extension occurs every time a request comes in to the server, the session's timeout will be extended automatically, ensuring that the session remains active as long as the user is interacting with the application.

Authorization mechanism

When we used sessions, every time we wanted to check if user is allowed to access, we wrote these lines:

```
var user = HttpContext.Session.Get<User>("UserContext");
if(user != null && user.Role == Role.Admin)
{

}
```

To make the authorization process simpler, we will use authorization attributes.

Custom authorization attributes

Custom authorization attributes allow you to define your own rules for authorizing access to controller actions. These attributes can be applied to controller actions.

```csharp
public class Auth(params Role[] roles) : Attribute, IAsyncActionFilter
{
  public Role[] Roles { get; set; } = roles;

  public async Task OnActionExecutionAsync(ActionExecutingContext context,
                          ActionExecutionDelegate next)
  {
    var user = context.HttpContext.Session.Get<User>("UserContext");

    if (Roles == null || Roles.Length == 0)
    {
        Decline(context);
    }
    if (user != null && (user.Role == Role.Admin || Roles.Contains(user.Role)))
    { await next(); }
    else { Decline(context); }
  }

  private void Decline(ActionExecutingContext context)
  {
      bool isView = true;

      if (isView)
      {
        context.Result = new RedirectToRouteResult(
              new RouteValueDictionary
              {
                { "action", "Error" },
                { "controller", "Home" },
                { "area", "" }
              });
      }
      else{
        context.Result = new JsonResult(new { Message = "Error" });
      }
  }
}
```

This code defines an attribute class named Auth, which implements IAsyncActionFilter.

Attribute Definition: The Auth class is defined as an attribute class. It inherits from Attribute and implements the IAsyncActionFilter interface. This means it can be applied as an attribute to controller actions.

Properties: Roles, this property holds an array of Role enum values. It's initialized through the constructor and is used to specify which roles are allowed to access the controller action.

OnActionExecutionAsync: This method is invoked before and after the execution of controller actions. It retrieves the User object from the session. Checks whether any roles are specified. If not, it immediately declines the request. If a user is logged in and their role is either Role.Admin or matches any of the specified roles, the request proceeds (next()). If the user is not logged in or doesn't have the required role, it declines the request by calling the Decline method.

Decline: This method is responsible for handling unauthorized access. It sets the result of the action to redirect to the error page if isView is true, otherwise it returns a JSON result with an error message.

This Auth attribute can be applied to controller actions to enforce authorization based on roles specified in the Roles property.

Use on controller

To use the Auth custom authorization attribute on the controller, you simply need to decorate the controller class with [Auth(Role.User)]. This will ensure that only users with the Role.User role can access any actions within the controller.

```
[Auth(Role.User)]
public class HomeController : Controller
{
}
```

Now, any action within the controller will require the user to have the Role.User role. If a user tries to access any action without this role, they will be redirected to the error page.

Use on action

```
public class HomeController : Controller
{

    [Auth(Role.User)]
    [HttpGet]
    public IActionResult Index()
    {
        return View();
```

```
    }

    [Auth(Role.Admin)]
    [HttpGet]
    public IActionResult AdminDashboard()
    {
        return View();
    }
}
```

The HomeController class has two action methods: Index and AdminDashboard.

The Index action is decorated with [Auth(Role.User)], meaning only users with the Role.User role can access this action.

The AdminDashboard action is decorated with [Auth(Role.Admin)], so only users with the Role.Admin role can access.

JWT

JWT, or JSON Web Token, is an open standard for securely transmitting information between two parties. It's like a special message with three parts.

Header: This defines the signing algorithm used (like a secret code) to verify the token's authenticity.

Payload: This is the most important part. It contains claims, which are pieces of information about the user, like their username, ID, or expiration time. This information is encoded in JSON format, which is human-readable.

Signature: This is a special code created by combining the header and payload with a secret key on the server-side. It ensures the information hasn't been tampered with during transmission.

JWTs are often used to make servers stateless in authentication processes. In traditional session-based authentication, the server needs to maintain a session state for each user, typically by storing session information in a database or memory cache. This approach can become a scalability bottleneck as the number of users increases because the server has to manage these session states. When using JWT, the server doesn't need to keep a record of tokens or sessions, as all the necessary information is contained within the token itself. However, since the information is visible to anyone who has access to the token, sensitive.

JWT vs Session

Feature	JWT	Session Table
Storage Location	Client-side (browser)	Server-side (database)
State	Stateless	Stateful
Scalability	More scalable	Less scalable
Performance	Better performance	Lower performance
API access	Well-suited for API access	Not ideal for API access
Security	Information potentially exposed on client-side	Information stored securely on server-side
Session Management	Less control over sessions	More control over sessions (invalidate, manage)
Data Updates	Less suitable for frequent data updates	More suitable for frequent data updates

Generate JWT token

Install package: Microsoft.AspNetCore.Authentication.JwtBearer

```csharp
public string GenerateJwtToken(
                Dictionary<string, string> values)
{
// Define the secret key used for signing the JWT
string jwtSecret = "4h#9@Fq7sN2Z1Kp3Wv6E5Xg8R4T0Y7lj";
byte[] jwtKey = Encoding.ASCII.GetBytes(jwtSecret);

// Initialize a JwtSecurityTokenHandler
var tokenHandler = new JwtSecurityTokenHandler();

// Create a SecurityTokenDescriptor which defines the
// token's payload and signing information
var tokenDescriptor = new SecurityTokenDescriptor
{
// Set the subject of the token, containing the claims
Subject = new ClaimsIdentity(values.Select(x => new Claim(x.Key, x.Value))),

// Set the expiration time of the token (1 day from now)
Expires = DateTime.UtcNow.AddDays(1),

// Set the signing credentials using a symmetric key and
// HMACSHA256 signature algorithm
SigningCredentials = new SigningCredentials(new SymmetricSecurityKey(jwtKey),
                SecurityAlgorithms.HmacSha256Signature)
};

// Create the JWT token based on the token descriptor
var token = tokenHandler.CreateToken(tokenDescriptor);

// Write the JWT token as a string
return tokenHandler.WriteToken(token);
}
```

This method takes in a dictionary of claims (key-value pairs), generates a JWT token with an expiration time of 1 day from now, and signs it using the provided secret key. Finally, it returns the generated JWT token as a string.

The minimum and maximum recommended lengths for the JWT secret key (jwtSecret) depend on the algorithm being used for signing the JWT.

For HMAC-SHA256, which is commonly used with JWT, the recommended minimum length is 256 bits (32 bytes). Longer keys generally provide stronger security, so a typical length for a JWT secret key would be 256 bits or longer.

There isn't a strict maximum length for the secret key, but it should be kept manageable for practical reasons such as storage and handling. Extremely long keys may introduce performance overhead and complexity without necessarily providing significant security benefits beyond a certain point.

```csharp
[HttpGet("login")]
public string Login(string? email, string? password)
{
    User user = GetUserFromDB(email, password);

    Dictionary<string, string> values = new() {
        {"UserId",user.UserId },
        {"Role",user.Role.ToString() }
    };

    return GenerateJwtToken(values);
}
```

Token result is:

eyJhbGciOiJIUzI1NiIsInR5cCI6IkpXVCJ9.eyJVc2VySWQiOiIxIiwiUm9sZSI6IkFkbWluIiwib mJmIjoxNzEwOTk1MDY5LCJleHAiOjE3MTEwODE0Njks ImlhdCI6MTcxMDk5NTA2OX0.c qqVlZoayT4SSc8w9tDxsDP9DVhMFbv5xo7X_P_Ci6k

Every time the client making a request to the server, he must send the token.

Let's create authorization middleware that decode the token

JwtToUserContextMiddleware

This middleware extracts a JWT token from the request's Authorization header, validates it, and extracts user information (UserId and Role) from the token's claims. It then stores this information in the HttpContext.Items collection, making it available to subsequent middleware or request handlers in the pipeline.

```csharp
public class JwtToUserContextMiddleware(
                    RequestDelegate next)
{
  public async Task InvokeAsync(HttpContext context)
  {
  // Extract the JWT token from the Authorization header
  context.Request.Headers.TryGetValue(HeaderNames.Authorization, out var jwt);

  // Check if a JWT token exists
  if (!string.IsNullOrEmpty(jwt))
  {
  // Validate the JWT token
  JwtSecurityToken jst = ValidateJwtToken(jwt);

  // Create a new User instance
  User u = new();

  // Extract the UserId claim from the JWT token and
  // assign it to the User instance
  u.UserId = jst.Claims.First(x => x.Type == "UserId").Value;

  // Extract the Role claim from the JWT token, parse it
  // to the Role enum, and assign it to the User instance
  u.Role = Enum.Parse<Role>(jst.Claims.First(x => x.Type == "Role").Value);

  // Store the User instance in the HttpContext Items
  // collection for later use
  context.Items["UserContext"] = u;
  }
  }



// Method to validate the JWT token
private JwtSecurityToken? ValidateJwtToken(string token)
{
  // Check if the token is null or empty
  if (string.IsNullOrEmpty(token))
      return null;
```

```csharp
// Initialize a JwtSecurityTokenHandler
var tokenHandler = new JwtSecurityTokenHandler();

// Define the secret key used to validate the token
string jwtSecret = "4h#9@Fq7sN2Z1Kp3Wv6E5Xg8R4T0Y7Ij";
byte[] jwtKey = Encoding.ASCII.GetBytes(jwtSecret);

// Validate the token using the provided parameters and
// retrieve the validated token
tokenHandler.ValidateToken(token, new TokenValidationParameters
  {
    ValidateIssuerSigningKey = true,
    IssuerSigningKey = new SymmetricSecurityKey(jwtKey),
    ValidateIssuer = false,
    ValidateAudience = false,
    ClockSkew = TimeSpan.Zero
  }, out SecurityToken validatedToken);

// Return the validated token as JwtSecurityToken
return (JwtSecurityToken)validatedToken;
  }
}
```

You can create an authorization attribute that checks if the HttpContext.Items collection contains the "UserContext" key.

Retrieve UserContext:

```csharp
[HttpGet("admin")]
public IActionResult Admin()
{
    var user = (User)HttpContext.Items["UserContext"];
}
```

Decode using JavaScript

JWT can be decoded using JavaScript because they are designed to be self-contained and easily parsed by client-side code.

JWT tokens are not encrypted by default, they are only signed. This means that the payload of the token is readable by anyone who has access to it.

The process of decoding a JWT token involves extracting the header, payload, and signature parts of the token and interpreting them. Here's how it works:

Base64 URL Decoding: The JWT token consists of three parts separated by dots ("."): the header, the payload, and the signature. Each part is Base64 URL encoded.

JSON Parsing: Once decoded, the header and payload parts are JSON strings.

Accessing Claims: The payload of the JWT token typically contains claims (information about the user or other data). After decoding and parsing, these claims can be accessed as properties of the JavaScript object representing the payload.

Signature Verification (Optional): While the payload can be decoded and accessed in JavaScript, the signature part cannot be verified solely on the client-side because it requires the secret key used by the server to sign the token. Signature verification is usually done on the server-side.

So, while decoding a JWT token can be done by anyone with access to the token, encoding (creating) and validating JWT tokens require access to the appropriate cryptographic functions and secret keys, which managed and controlled by the server-side code.

So, in short, every person can decode JWT tokens, but only authorized server-side entities can encode new tokens and validate existing ones.

```javascript
const jwtToken =
'eyJhbGciOiJIUzI1NiIsInR5cCI6IkpXVCJ9.eyJVc2VySWQiOiIxIiwiUm9sZSI6IkFkbWluIiwibmJmIj
oxNzEwOTk1MDY5LCJleHAiOjE3MTEwODE0NjksImlhdCI6MTcxMDk5NTA2OX0.cqqVlZoayT4SSc8w9tDxsD
P9DVhMFbv5xo7X_P_Ci6k';

// Split the token into its three parts
const parts = jwtToken.split('.');

// Decode each part using Base64 decoding
const header = JSON.parse(atob(parts[0]));
const payload = JSON.parse(atob(parts[1]));
const signature = parts[2]; // No need to decode signature

// Output the decoded parts
console.log("Header:", header);
console.log("Payload:", payload);
console.log("Signature:", signature);
```

Header: ▶ *{alg: 'HS256', typ: 'JWT'}*

Payload: ▶ *{UserId: '1', Role: 'Admin', nbf: 1710995069, exp: 1711081469, iat: 1710995069}*

Signature: cqqVlZoayT4SSc8w9tDxsDP9DVhMFbv5xo7X_P_Ci6k

JWT Issues

Security Risks if Not Handled Properly: JWTs can be tampered with if the secret key used to sign them is compromised. This could potentially lead to security vulnerabilities, such as unauthorized access to protected resources or injection attacks.

Token Expiration: JWTs can have expiration times, but if not implemented properly, expired tokens might still be accepted, leading to security risks. Refresh tokens are often used alongside JWTs to mitigate this issue, allowing the generation of new JWTs without requiring the user to re-authenticate.

Token Size: Since JWTs contain encoded data, including user claims and other information, they can become large, especially when storing a lot of user-related data in the payload. Transmitting large JWTs can impact network performance and increase latency.

Limited Revocation Solutions

Unlike traditional session-based authentication systems, JWTs are stateless. Once issued, they cannot be revoked or invalidated before their expiration time.

Limited revocation in token-based authentication systems, particularly with JWTs and refresh tokens, poses challenges due to the stateless nature of these tokens. However, there are several strategies and solutions to mitigate the risks associated with limited revocation:

Short Token Lifetimes: Implement short lifetimes for both access tokens and refresh tokens. By reducing the lifespan of tokens, the window of vulnerability in case of token compromise is minimized. Short-lived tokens also necessitate more frequent refreshes, limiting the impact of any potential compromise.

Token Blacklisting: Maintain a blacklist of revoked tokens on the server side. When a token needs to be revoked, add its identifier to the blacklist. During token validation, check if the token is blacklisted before accepting it. While effective, this approach requires additional storage and management overhead. Using Redis database for token blacklisting can be a highly efficient solution, as Redis is an in-memory data store that excels at fast read and write operations

Token Rotation: Implement token rotation mechanisms, where tokens are regularly refreshed and replaced with new tokens. This helps mitigate the risk of long-lived tokens being compromised. With token rotation, even if a token is compromised, its lifespan is limited until the next rotation occurs.

Usage of Refresh Tokens with Short Lifespans: Refresh tokens typically have longer lifespans than access tokens. However, consider using refresh tokens with shorter lifespans to minimize the window of vulnerability. Additionally, refresh tokens can be invalidated and replaced during token rotation or when user permissions change.

Token Revocation Endpoints: Implement token revocation endpoints that allow clients to explicitly revoke tokens. When a user logs out or their permissions change, clients can call this endpoint to revoke associated tokens. This approach provides more control over token revocation but requires proper authentication and authorization mechanisms for token revocation requests.

Refresh Tokens

When a user makes a login request, a unique token called a refresh token is created, with a longer expiration date than the JWT token. This refresh token is then stored in the database alongside the user's information, and it's returned to the client along with the JWT token.

When the JWT token expires, the user sends a refresh token request containing the refresh token. If the refresh token exists in the database and has a valid expiration date, a new JWT token is created.

So, why not simply save the Refresh JWT Date instead of storing two fields in the database, the token and its expiration date? The reason lies in the flexibility it offers. By storing both the token and its expiration date, you gain the ability to manage multiple refresh tokens for the same user across various devices.

This approach allows for distinct refresh tokens to be associated with different devices, granting granular control over user sessions. For instance, if a user logs in from multiple devices simultaneously, each device can be assigned its own refresh token. Consequently, if access needs to be revoked for one particular device, you can simply invalidate the corresponding refresh token associated with it, without affecting other active sessions.

OAuth2

OAuth2 is an authorization framework that lets applications access resources on behalf of a user, without getting their password. It's very similar to JWT but without that data inside the token.

It's commonly used with services like Google, where you can sign into an app or website (like a forum) by clicking "Sign in with Google" instead of creating a new account manually.

When you click the Google button, Google shows you a consent screen, and if you approve, it generates an authorization code which the app exchanges for an access token. The token allows the app to access only the data you approved, such as your name or email, without ever seeing your Google password.

Step 1: Authorization Request (User → Authorization Server)

Your app redirects the user to: https://authorization-server.com/oauth/authorize

Required Query Parameters:

Field	Description	Example
response_type	Must be "code"	code
client_id	Your app's public identifier	abc123
redirect_uri	Where to redirect after login	https://yourapp.com/callback
scope	What access you want	email profile
state	(Recommended) CSRF protection token	xyz987

Step 2: Token Request (Your Server → Authorization Server)

After receiving the code, your server sends a POST to:

https://authorization-server.com/oauth/token

Required x-www-form-urlencoded Body:

Field	Description	Example
grant_type	Must be "authorization_code"	authorization_code
code	The auth code you received	AbCdEf123456
redirect_uri	Must match the original redirect URI	https://yourapp.com/callback
client_id	Your app's public ID	abc123
client_secret	Your app's private secret	shhh-its-a-secret

Step 3: Token Response (You get this from the server)

If successful, you'll receive:

```
{
    access_token: " some-token
    token_type: "Bearer",
    expires_in: 3600,
    refresh_token: "some-refresh-token",
    scope: "email profile"
}
```

Authorization header types

The Authorization HTTP header is used to provide credentials for authenticating a user agent with a server.

There are several common types (schemes) for the Authorization header:

Type	Example Authorization Header	Common?	Notes
Basic	Basic Zm9vOmJhcg==	High	base64(username:password)
Bearer	Bearer eyJhbGciOiJI...	High	Often JWT
Digest	Digest username=...	Low	Old, legacy servers
AWS	AWS4-HMAC-SHA256 ...	Medium	Cloud APIs
OAuth 1	OAuth oauth_consumer_key=...	Low	Old APIs
ApiKey	ApiKey 12345	Medium	API access key
Token	Token 12345	Low	Not standard
Custom	MyCustomScheme xyz	Low	Private/internal APIs
Negotiate	Negotiate ...	Low	Windows SSO

The most used authorization headers are:

API Key – Unique key for client atuntication, sometimes in the Authorization header, but often as its own header (like x-api-key).

Format: Authorization: ApiKey <your-key> or X-API-KEY: <your-key>

Basic - The credentials are username:password encoded in Base64. From security perspective it's not encrypted, use only with HTTPS!

Format: Authorization: Basic <base64-encoded-credentials>

Bearer - The token is usually a JWT (JSON Web Token), but can be any string representing the user's session/authorization.

Format: Authorization: Bearer <token>

Load Balancer

A load balancer is a component in distributed systems. It acts as an intermediary between clients and backend servers, distributing incoming network traffic across multiple servers to ensure optimal resource utilization, reliability, and scalability.

Here's an overview of load balancers and their functions:

Traffic Distribution: Load balancers evenly distribute incoming network traffic (e.g., HTTP requests) across multiple backend servers. This prevents any single server from becoming overloaded, ensuring consistent performance and responsiveness for users.

Health Monitoring: Load balancers continually monitor the health and availability of backend servers by periodically sending health checks (e.g., ICMP pings, HTTP requests). If a server becomes unavailable or unhealthy, the load balancer stops routing traffic to it, thereby improving reliability and fault tolerance.

Session Persistence: In scenarios where maintaining session state is necessary (e.g., for web applications with user sessions), load balancers can support session persistence (sticky sessions). This ensures that subsequent requests from the same client are routed to the same backend server, preserving session data and improving user experience.

SSL Termination: Load balancers can offload SSL/TLS encryption and decryption tasks from backend servers, improving performance by reducing the computational burden on server resources.

Scalability: Load balancers enable horizontal scaling of applications by seamlessly adding or removing backend servers based on demand. This elasticity allows applications to handle increasing traffic loads without downtime or degradation in performance.

Content-Based Routing: Advanced load balancers can route traffic based on content attributes (e.g., URL path, HTTP headers), enabling more sophisticated traffic management strategies such as A/B testing, blue-green deployments, or canary releases.

Distributed Denial of Service (DDoS) Mitigation: Load balancers can mitigate DDoS attacks by filtering and scrubbing malicious traffic before it reaches backend servers, protecting the infrastructure from service disruptions.

Compression

You can enable compression to reduce the size of data sent between the server and the client, thus improving performance. Compression is particularly useful for reducing the load time of web pages and improving the overall user experience.

Keep in mind that not all content benefits equally from compression, and the effectiveness of compression depends on the nature of the content being served. Always test and monitor the impact of compression on your application's performance.

Gzip

Gzip (short for GNU zip) is a widely used data compression algorithm and file format. It was developed as part of the GNU project and is commonly employed for compressing and decompressing files and data streams. Gzip is particularly prevalent in web development, where it is often used to compress web content before transmission over the network.

Gzip is commonly used to compress web content, including HTML, CSS, JavaScript, and other text-based files. Compressing these files before sending them to the client reduces the amount of data that needs to be transferred over the network, improving website performance and load times.

Gzip uses the ".gz" file extension for compressed files. When a file is compressed with Gzip, its size is reduced, and the ".gz" extension is appended to the original filename (e.g., "example.html" becomes "example.html.gz").

HTTP Compression: Gzip is supported by most web browsers and web servers. When a web server is configured to use Gzip compression, it includes the "Content-Encoding: gzip" header in the HTTP response. This informs the browser that the content is compressed, and the browser then decompresses it before rendering.

Gzip is based on the DEFLATE compression algorithm, which is a combination of LZ77 (Lempel–Ziv 1977) and Huffman coding. The DEFLATE algorithm is a widely used compression algorithm, and the Gzip format is specified in several RFCs (Request for Comments), making it an open standard.

Brotli

Brotli is a data compression algorithm developed by Google. It is designed to be more efficient than existing compression algorithms, such as gzip and deflate, in terms of both compression ratio and compression speed. Brotli is particularly well-suited for compressing web content like HTML, CSS, and JavaScript.

While Brotli achieves better compression ratios, it may have a slightly higher compression time compared to gzip. However, the trade-off is usually considered worthwhile, especially for scenarios where bandwidth savings are crucial.

Brotli can be applied to various types of files, but it is particularly effective for compressing text-based files such as HTML, CSS, JavaScript, and JSON.

How to use?

Program.cs

```csharp
builder.Services.AddResponseCompression(options =>
{
    // Enable compression for HTTPS requests
    options.EnableForHttps = true;

    //Add Gzip compression to the services.
    options.Providers.Add<GzipCompressionProvider>();

    //Add Brotli compression to the services.
    options.Providers.Add<BrotliCompressionProvider>();
});

// Enable both Brotli and Gzip compression middleware
app.UseResponseCompression();
```

The default behavior of app.UseResponseCompression() is to use the built-in compression providers (GzipCompressionProvider and BrotliCompressionProvider)

So, no need to add them to ResponseCompressionOptions.

If you enable both Gzip and Brotli compression in your application, the server will utilize content negotiation to decide which compression algorithm to use for a particular response. Content negotiation occurs based on the client's capabilities, as indicated by the Accept-Encoding header in the HTTP request.

Client Request

The client sends an HTTP request to the server, including an Accept-Encoding header specifying the compression algorithms it supports, such as "gzip, br".

Server Decision

The server receives the request and looks at the Accept-Encoding header.

If the client supports both Gzip and Brotli, the server decides which compression algorithm to use based on factors such as server configuration, resource availability, and possibly the compression efficiency of each algorithm.

Compression

The server compresses the response using the chosen compression algorithm (either Gzip or Brotli).

The Content-Encoding header is set in the HTTP response to indicate the compression method used.

Client Decompression

The client receives the compressed response and decompresses it using the supported compression algorithm.

By enabling both compression algorithms, your server is more flexible in accommodating a variety of clients with different capabilities. Modern browsers often support both Gzip and Brotli, and their support is indicated in the Accept-Encoding header. The server can choose the compression method that provides the best compression ratio while considering factors like server load and resource availability.

It's important to note that the effectiveness of compression depends on the nature of the content being served. Some content may compress better with Gzip, while other content may benefit more from Brotli. Enabling both provides a good balance for different scenarios.

Always test and monitor the performance of your application with both compression algorithms enabled to ensure that it meets your performance goals and does not introduce unexpected issues.

Logs

Logging is the process of recording events, activities, or messages during the execution of a program or operation. Logging is crucial for various reasons, including debugging, troubleshooting, monitoring, and auditing. It helps developers and system administrators understand what happened within a system, identify issues, and track the flow of execution.

Debugging and Troubleshooting: Developers use logs to track the flow of their programs and identify issues during development and testing.

When unexpected errors occur, logs provide valuable information about the state of the application at the time of the error, helping developers diagnose and fix problems.

Monitoring and Performance Analysis: System administrators use logs to monitor the health and performance of a system.

By analyzing logs, administrators can identify patterns, spot anomalies, and optimize system performance.

Security and Auditing: Logs play a crucial role in security by recording events related to user authentication, access control, and potential security breaches.

They are essential for auditing purposes, helping organizations comply with regulations and investigate security incidents.

ILogger

.NET provides a built-in logging infrastructure. The ILogger<T> interface is a generic interface that allows you to perform logging in your application while providing the category of the logger (typically the class or component name). By default, when you use ILogger, log messages will be printed to the console. This provides a convenient way to quickly view log output during development and debugging.

```csharp
[ApiController]
[Route("")]
public class HomeController(ILogger<HomeController> logger) : ControllerBase
{
    [HttpGet("index")]
    public void Index()
    {
        logger.LogInformation("Hello");
    }
}
```

```
}
```

```
info: WebApplication1.Controllers.HomeController[0]
      Hello
```

Logging levels

The ILogger<T> interface provides methods for different logging levels.

Different logging levels provide a way to categorize and prioritize log messages based on their significance. They help in debugging, monitoring, and addressing issues efficiently.

Level	Purpose	Usage
Trace	Most detailed messages, often for granular debugging	Disabled by default, use only in development or troubleshooting
Debug	Detailed information for debugging and development	Use with caution in production due to high volume
Information	General tracking of application flow	Useful for monitoring and long-term analysis
Warning	Abnormal events or conditions that don't cause immediate failure	Indicate potential issues for further investigation
Error	Unhandled errors or exceptions that affect current operations	Signal failures that require attention and potentially corrective action
Critical	Severe failures that demand urgent intervention	Examples: data loss, system crashes, out-of-disk-space scenarios
None	Disables logging for a specific category	Suppresses messages from the designated category

```
logger.LogInformation("Hello");

logger.LogWarning("Hello");

logger.LogError("Hello");

logger.LogCritical("Hello");

//logger.LogTrace("Hello");

//logger.LogDebug("Hello");
```

```
info: WebApplication1.Controllers.HomeController[0]
      Hello
warn: WebApplication1.Controllers.HomeController[0]
      Hello
fail: WebApplication1.Controllers.HomeController[0]
      Hello
crit: WebApplication1.Controllers.HomeController[0]
      Hello
```

You can pass an exception along with a log message.

```
logger.LogError(ex, "An error occurred");
```

Configuration

In .NET application, the appsettings.json file is commonly used to store configuration settings for various components, including logging. The logging configuration in appsettings.json defines how the application should handle log messages, including the minimum log level, log levels for specific categories, and other logging-related settings.

appsettings.json

```json
{
  "Logging": {
    "LogLevel": {
      "Default": "Information",
      "Microsoft.AspNetCore": "Warning"
    }
  },
  "AllowedHosts": "*",
}
```

Logging Section: The top-level "Logging" section contains all logging-related configurations.

LogLevel Property: The "LogLevel" property is a sub-section that allows you to configure the minimum log level for different categories.

Default Level: "Default": "Information" sets the default minimum log level for all categories. In this example, messages with a severity level of "Information" or higher will be captured by default.

Microsoft.AspNetCore Category: "Microsoft.AspNetCore": "Warning" sets the minimum log level specifically for the "Microsoft.AspNetCore" category. In this case, only messages with a severity level of "Warning" or higher from this category will be captured.

Log Scope

Logging scopes allow you to enrich log messages with contextual information, making it easier to trace the flow of your application or diagnose issues within a specific context. Scopes provide a way to group related log messages together, and they are especially useful in scenarios where the same logger is shared across multiple operations.

```
[ApiController]
[Route("")]
public class HomeController(ILogger<HomeController> logger) : ControllerBase
{
    [HttpGet("index")]
    public void Index()
    {
        using (logger.BeginScope("Index"))
        {
            logger.LogInformation("start");
            Logic();
            logger.LogInformation("end");
        }
    }

    [NonAction]
    public void Logic()
    {
        using (logger.BeginScope("Logic"))
        logger.LogInformation("start");
    }
}
```

Program.cs

```
builder.Services.AddLogging(builder =>
{
    builder.AddSimpleConsole(opts => {
        opts.IncludeScopes = true;
        opts.SingleLine = true;
    });
});
```

```
info: WebApplication1.Controllers.HomeController[0] =>
SpanId:34c98572611aed5c, TraceId:3a3eb4fe5a17fd8da1c389
ba5e135482, ParentId:0000000000000000 => ConnectionId:0
HN0ES42NU56M => RequestPath:/index RequestId:0HN0ES42NU
56M:00000009 => WebApplication1.Controllers.HomeControl
ler.Index (WebApplication1) => Index start
info: WebApplication1.Controllers.HomeController[0] =>
SpanId:34c98572611aed5c, TraceId:3a3eb4fe5a17fd8da1c389
ba5e135482, ParentId:0000000000000000 => ConnectionId:0
HN0ES42NU56M => RequestPath:/index RequestId:0HN0ES42NU
56M:00000009 => WebApplication1.Controllers.HomeControl
ler.Index (WebApplication1) => Index => Logic start
info: WebApplication1.Controllers.HomeController[0] =>
SpanId:34c98572611aed5c, TraceId:3a3eb4fe5a17fd8da1c389
ba5e135482, ParentId:0000000000000000 => ConnectionId:0
HN0ES42NU56M => RequestPath:/index RequestId:0HN0ES42NU
56M:00000009 => WebApplication1.Controllers.HomeControl
ler.Index (WebApplication1) => Index end
```

In each of the log entries, you can observe a string that indicates the current function context, such as the Index function and Logic function.

ILoggerProvider

ILoggerProvider allows you to create a custom logging provider.

```csharp
// Define a custom logging provider
class InfraLoggerProvider(ServiceProvider serviceProvider) : ILoggerProvider
{
    // Creates an instance of InfraLogger
    public ILogger CreateLogger(string categoryName)
    {
        return new InfraLogger(categoryName, serviceProvider);
    }


    public void Dispose(){} // Implementation of IDisposable if dispse needed
}

// Define a custom logger
public sealed class InfraLogger : ILogger
{
    public InfraLogger(string name){}

    public IDisposable? BeginScope<TState>(TState state)
                where TState : notnull => default!;

    public bool IsEnabled(LogLevel logLevel) => true;

    // Implementation of Log method
    public void Log<TState>(LogLevel logLevel, EventId eventId, TState state,
        Exception? exception, Func<TState, Exception?, string> formatter)
    {
        // Check if logging is enabled for the specified log level
        if (!IsEnabled(logLevel)) { return; }

        // Custom logs saving in files
        string folder = $@"C:\Logs\";
        if (!Directory.Exists(folder))
            Directory.CreateDirectory(folder);
```

```
        Task.Run(async () => {
          await File.AppendAllTextAsync($"{folder}
          {DateTime.Now:dd_MM_yyyy HH}.txt",
           $"{DateTime.Now:dd/MM/yyyy HH:mm:ss.fff} –
          {logLevel}-log: {formatter(state, exception)}");
        });
      }
}
```

Program.cs

```
// Add the InfraLoggerProvider to the logging providers
srv.AddLogging(builder =>
{
    builder.AddProvider(new InfraLoggerProvider(
            builder.Services.BuildServiceProvider()));
});
```

Localization

Localization involves adapting the content of a web application to different languages and regions. ASP.NET provides several features and techniques to support localization

RESX file

A RESX file, or Resource file is used to store resources such as strings and other data that need to be localized or managed separately from the code. These files have the extension ".resx". A RESX file is essentially an XML-based file that stores key-value pairs, where the keys represent identifiers for resources, and the values represent the actual resource data.

Create empty Resource class.

Create 2 resx files in Resources folder:

Resource.resx

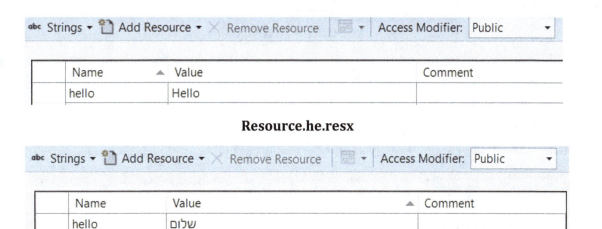

Resource.he.resx

Name	Value	Comment
hello	שלום	

Change the access modifier of each file to public.

In this structure, Resource.resx is the default resource file containing your strings in the default language (e.g., English), and Resource.he.resx is the resource file containing hebrew translations.

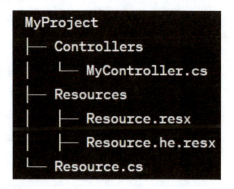

```
MyProject
├── Controllers
│   └── MyController.cs
├── Resources
│   ├── Resource.resx
│   ├── Resource.he.resx
└── Resource.cs
```

Access Modifier

The access modifier determines the accessibility of the generated code class associated with the RESX file.

Internal: The generated code class is accessible only within the same assembly (project). Other assemblies cannot directly access the resources defined in this class.

Public: The generated code class becomes accessible from other assemblies. This means that other assemblies can reference and use the resources defined in this class.

No Code Generation: By default, Visual Studio auto-generates a code-behind class for RESX files, making it easier to access resources in your code through strongly-typed properties. However, in some scenarios, you may want to avoid this auto-generation and directly access the resources without relying on generated code.

IStringLocalizer

IStringLocalizer is an interface that is used for localization in applications. IStringLocalizer provides a way to retrieve localized strings based on the current culture or specified culture.

```csharp
[Route("")][ApiController]
public class MyController(IStringLocalizer<Resource> localizer) :ControllerBase
{
    [HttpGet("getString")]
    public void GetString()
    {
        string str = localizer["hello"];
    }
}
```

localizer["hello"] is used to retrieve a localized string with the key "hello" from the resource file associated with the Resource class.

Program.cs

```csharp
builder.Services.AddLocalization(options => options.ResourcesPath = "Resources");
```

ResourcesPath property: Determines the path where the application will search for resource files containing localized content.

```csharp
[HttpGet("getString")]
0 references
public void GetString()
{
    string str = localizer["hello"];
} ≤ 179,274ms elapse  ◈ str    🔍 View ▾ "שלום" ⊡
```

Culture

With CultureInfo, you can set the current language (culture) for your application.

```
public class CultureMiddleware(RequestDelegate next)
{
 public async Task InvokeAsync(HttpContext context)
 {
   context.Request.Headers.TryGetValue("lang", out var lang);
   CultureInfo culture;

   if (lang == "en")
   {
     culture = new CultureInfo("e`n-US");
   }
   else
   {
     culture = new CultureInfo("he-IL");
   }
   CultureInfo.CurrentCulture = CultureInfo.CurrentUICulture = culture;

   await next(context);
 }
}
```

This middleware intercepts each incoming request, retrieves the value of the lang header, and sets the current culture accordingly. If the lang header is "en", it sets the culture to English (United States), otherwise, it sets it to Hebrew (Israel).

Custom IStringLocalizer

JsonLocalizer class is a custom implementation of the IStringLocalizer. It's designed to load localized strings from JSON files and provide them to your application based on the current culture.

```
public class JsonLocalizer : IStringLocalizer
{
 private readonly Dictionary<string, Dictionary<string, string>>
```

```csharp
                        localizedStringsDic;
public JsonLocalizer()
{
  localizedStringsDic = new Dictionary<string, Dictionary<string, string>>();


  // Specify the path to the directory containing the JSON files
  var jsonDirectory = Path.Combine(
    AppDomain.CurrentDomain.BaseDirectory, "Resources");


  // Load localized strings from JSON files
  LoadLocalizedStrings(jsonDirectory);
}
private void LoadLocalizedStrings(string jsonDirectory)
{
  // Get all JSON files in the directory
  var jsonFiles = Directory.GetFiles(jsonDirectory, "Lang.*.json");


  foreach (var jsonFile in jsonFiles)
  {
   // Extract culture name from the file name
   var cultureName = Path.GetFileNameWithoutExtension(jsonFile)
                                    .Split('.')[1];


  // Read JSON content and deserialize it
   var jsonContent = File.ReadAllText(jsonFile);
   var file = jsonContent.Deserialize<Dictionary<string,string>>();


   // Add the localized strings to the dictionary
   localizedStringsDic[cultureName] = file;
  }
}


public LocalizedString this[string name] => GetString(name);


public LocalizedString this[string name, params object[] arguments] =>
                           GetString(name, arguments);


public IEnumerable<LocalizedString> GetAllStrings(bool includeParentCultures)
{
    throw new NotImplementedException();
```
180

```
        }

        private LocalizedString GetString(string name, params object[] arguments)
        {
            string lang = CultureInfo.CurrentCulture.TwoLetterISOLanguageName;

            if (localizedStringsDic.TryGetValue(lang, out var localizedStrings))
            {
                if (localizedStrings.TryGetValue(name, out var value))
                {
                    if (arguments != null && arguments.Length > 0)
                    {
                        value = string.Format(value, arguments);
                    }
                    return new LocalizedString(name, value);
                }
            }
            return new LocalizedString(name, name, true);
        }
    }
```

Create 2 jsons files in Resources folder:

Lang.en.json

```
{ "hello": "Hello" }
```

Lang.he.json

```
{ "hello": "שלום" }
```

Add the custom Localizer:

Program.cs

```
services.AddSingleton<IStringLocalizer, JsonLocalizer>();
```

Use the localizer:

```
[Route("")][ApiController]
public class MyController(IStringLocalizer localizer) : ControllerBase
{
    [HttpGet("getString")]
```

```
    public void GetString()
    {
        string str = localizer["hello"];
    }
}
```

CORS

Cross-Origin Resource Sharing (CORS) is a security feature implemented by web browsers to prevent unauthorized access to resources hosted on a different origin (domain, protocol, or port) than the one from which the web page originated. CORS defines a mechanism that allows servers to specify which origins are permitted to access their resources, thus enabling controlled sharing of resources across different origins.

Same-Origin Policy (SOP): Browsers enforce the Same-Origin Policy by default, which restricts web pages from making requests to resources hosted on a different origin. This policy helps prevent malicious websites from accessing sensitive data from other origins.

Cross-Origin Requests: Cross-origin requests occur when a web page makes a request to a resource located on a different origin than the one from which the page originated. These requests are subject to CORS restrictions imposed by the server hosting the resource.

CORS Headers: CORS is implemented through HTTP headers exchanged between the client (browser) and the server. The main CORS headers include:

Access-Control-Allow-Origin: Specifies which origins are allowed to access the resource.

Access-Control-Allow-Methods: Specifies which HTTP methods are allowed for the resource.

Access-Control-Allow-Headers: Specifies which headers are allowed in the request.

Access-Control-Allow-Credentials: Indicates whether the browser should include credentials (such as cookies or authorization headers) in the request.

Access-Control-Expose-Headers: Specifies which headers the browser is allowed to access in the response.

Access-Control-Max-Age: Specifies how long the results of a preflight request (OPTIONS) can be cached.

Preflight Requests: Before making certain cross-origin requests (such as requests with custom headers or methods other than GET, POST, or HEAD), the browser sends a preflight OPTIONS request to the server to determine if the actual request is safe to send. The server responds with CORS headers indicating whether the request is allowed.

Credentials and Cookies: By default, browsers do not include credentials (such as cookies or HTTP authentication) in cross-origin requests. To allow credentials to be sent, both the client and server must opt-in by setting the withCredentials property on the XMLHttpRequest object (or credentials in Fetch API) and configuring the server to allow credentials using the Access-Control-Allow-Credentials header.

Server Configuration: In server-side applications, CORS policies can be configured to control which origins, methods, headers, and credentials are allowed to access resources.

By default, in asp.net CORS is disabled. When CORS is disabled, attempting to make an HTTP request to your server at the address api.eldarbooks.com from JavaScript code within a browser with a domain that is different from api.eldarbooks.com will result in a CORS error. The browser sends an OPTIONS HTTP request to your server, and if the server responds with a 200 status code, the browser will then send the intended request.

To enable CORS:

```
services.AddCors(options =>
{
    options.AddDefaultPolicy(builder =>
    {
      var arr = new [] { "eldarbooks.com","eldarsite.com" };

      builder
      .WithOrigins(arr) // use SetIsOriginAllowed(origin => true) to allow all
      .AllowAnyMethod()
      .AllowAnyHeader()
      .AllowCredentials();
    });
});

app.UseCors();
```

services.AddCors(options => { ... }): This line configures CORS services in the application. It registers the CORS middleware and specifies how CORS policies should be configured.

options.AddDefaultPolicy(builder => { ... }): This line adds a default CORS policy. The AddDefaultPolicy method creates a default CORS policy that applies to all requests if no other policy matches.

var arr = new[] { "https://eldarbooks.com", "https://eldarsite.com" }: This line defines an array of allowed origins. Origins are URLs from which requests are allowed to originate.

.WithOrigins(allowedOrigins): This line specifies the allowed origins for the CORS policy. The WithOrigins method sets the origins that are allowed to access the resources.

.AllowAnyMethod(): This line allows any HTTP method (GET, POST, PUT, DELETE, etc.) for CORS requests. The AllowAnyMethod method configures the policy to allow any HTTP method for requests.

.AllowAnyHeader(): This line allows any HTTP headers in CORS requests. The AllowAnyHeader method configures the policy to allow any headers to be included in requests.

.AllowCredentials(): This line indicates that the CORS policy allows credentials to be included in cross-origin requests. The AllowCredentials method configures the policy to allow credentials (such as cookies or authorization headers) to be sent with requests.

Custom policy

To define a custom CORS policy with specific configurations, you can use the AddPolicy method instead of AddDefaultPolicy. This allows you to create multiple custom CORS policies and apply them to different endpoints or controllers as needed.

```
services.AddCors(options =>
{
    options.AddPolicy("MyCustomPolicy", builder => {
        builder
            .WithOrigins("https://example.com").AllowAnyMethod()
            .WithHeaders("Content-Type", "Authorization").AllowCredentials();
    });
});


app.UseCors("MyCustomPolicy");
```

[EnableCors]

The [EnableCors] attribute is used to apply a specific CORS policy to an individual controller or action method.

```
[EnableCors("MyCustomPolicy")]
public class MyController : ControllerBase
{
    [HttpGet]public IActionResult Get(){ return Ok(); }
```

Content Security Policy (CSP)

CSP stands for Content Security Policy. It's a security feature that helps prevent cross-site scripting (XSS), data injection, and other types of code injection attacks in web applications. CSP works by letting a website owner tell the browser which content sources are trusted. This is done using a special HTTP response header, like this:

Content-Security-Policy: default-src 'self'; script-src 'self' https://trusted.com

This policy tells the browser:

Only load scripts from the website itself ('self') and from https://trusted.com

Block all other scripts, even if an attacker tries to inject them

```
app.Use(async (context, next) =>
{
    context.Response.Headers.Add("Content-Security-Policy",
        "default-src 'self'; script-src 'self' https://trusted.com");
    await next();
});
```

CORS VS CSP

Aspect	CORS (Cross-Origin Resource Sharing)	CSP (Content Security Policy)
Purpose	Controls **which external origins** can make HTTP requests to your server.	Controls **which sources** the browser is allowed to load content from.
Who enforces?	Browser enforces based on server's HTTP headers.	Browser enforces based on server's HTTP headers.
Scope	Applies to **cross-origin HTTP requests** (e.g., AJAX/fetch calls).	Applies to **loading of resources** (scripts, styles, images, frames, etc.) inside the page.
Goal	Prevent unauthorized cross-origin requests (protect server data).	Prevent malicious or unauthorized content injection in the page (protect user/browser).
Main header(s)	`Access-Control-Allow-Origin` and related CORS headers.	`Content-Security-Policy` header.
Example scenario	Your frontend app on `https://myapp.com` fetches data from `https://api.com`. You allow it via CORS.	Your website wants to block loading scripts from unknown or dangerous domains to prevent XSS attacks.
Controls	Who can make requests to your API or server.	What resources the browser loads and executes on your page.

In both CORS and CSP, the browser (like Chrome, Firefox, Edge) is the one that enforces the rules and blocks unauthorized or unsafe content.

Feature	Who sets the policy?	Who enforces the policy?	What gets blocked?
CORS	The **server** sends headers like `Access-Control-Allow-Origin`	The **browser** checks the server's response and blocks requests if not allowed	Cross-origin HTTP requests (AJAX, fetch, fonts, etc.) that violate the policy
CSP	The **server** sends the `Content-Security-Policy` header	The **browser** blocks loading or executing resources not allowed by the policy	Scripts, styles, images, frames, inline code, etc. that violate the policy

Network protocols

Network protocols are sets of rules that govern communication between devices over a network. These protocols define how data is formatted, transmitted, received, and acknowledged across the network. They ensure that devices can understand each other and effectively exchange information.

SmtpClient

Simple Mail Transfer Protocol (SMTP): is an application-layer protocol used for sending email messages between mail servers.

SmtpClient is a class that enables you to send email messages using SMTP.

```csharp
using System.Net.Mail;
using System.Net;

// Class to represent the email request
public class EmailRequest
{
    //Indicates if the email body is HTML
    public bool IsHtml { get; set; }

    //Body of the email
    public string Body { get; set; }

    //Subject of the email
    public string Subject { get; set; }

    //Sender's email address
    public string FromEmail { get; set; }

    //Recipient's email address
    public string ToEmail { get; set; }

    //Sender's SMTP email address
    public string SmtpEmail { get; set; }

    //Sender's SMTP password
```

```csharp
    public string SmtpPassword { get; set; }

    // Paths to files
    public List<string> FilesPath { get; set; }
}
```

```csharp
public class EmailSvc
{
    // Method to send email asynchronously
    public async Task Send(EmailRequest r)
    {
        // Create and configure the SMTP client
        using var smtp = new SmtpClient
        {
            // SMTP server host (Gmail in this case)
            Host = "smtp.gmail.com",

            // Port number for SMTP (587 for Gmail)
            Port = 587,

            // Enable SSL/TLS encryption for secure communication
            EnableSsl = true,

            // Specify delivery method as Network
            DeliveryMethod = SmtpDeliveryMethod.Network,

            // Provide credentials for SMTP authentication
            Credentials = new NetworkCredential(r.SmtpEmail, r.SmtpPassword),

            // Set timeout for the operation (in milliseconds)
            Timeout = 20000
        };

        // Create MailMessage object with sender and recipient addresses
        using var message = new MailMessage(r.FromEmail, r.ToEmail)
        {

            // Set the subject of the email message
            Subject = r.Subject,

            // Set the body of the email message
            Body = r.Body,

            // Specify whether the body of the email is HTML or plain text
            IsBodyHtml = r.IsHtml
        };
```

190

```csharp
        // Attach files to the email message, if any
        if (r.FilesPath?.Count > 0)
        {
            foreach (var path in r.FilesPath)
            {
                message.Attachments.Add(new Attachment(path));
            }
        }

        // Send the email asynchronously
        await smtp.SendMailAsync(message);
    }
}
```

Send email with html and files:

```csharp
public class MyService(EmailSvc emailSvc)
{
    public async Task SendEmail()
    {
        var emailRequest = new EmailRequest
        {
            IsHtml = true,
            Body = "<html><body><h1>Hello, World!</h1></body></html>",
            Subject = "Test Email",
            FromEmail = "sender@gmail.com",
            ToEmail = "recipient@example.com",
            SmtpEmail = "sender@gmail.com",
            SmtpPassword = "password",
            FilesPath = new List<string> { "filepath1.txt", "filepath2.pdf" }
        };

        await emailSvc.Send(emailRequest);
    }
}
```

HTTPClient

HTTP is an application-layer protocol used for transmitting hypermedia documents, such as HTML pages and Json's, over the World Wide Web.

HttpClient is a class that provides functionality to send HTTP requests and receive HTTP responses from a specified URI (Uniform Resource Identifier).

Let's create a RestSvc class that provides a method SendAsync for sending asynchronous HTTP requests, including timeout management, retry mechanisms, and support for deserialization.

The AddHttpClient() method is used to register the HttpClient service with the dependency injection container. This registration allows you to inject HttpClient instances into your application's components.

Program.cs

```csharp
builder.Services.AddHttpClient();
```

```csharp
using Microsoft.Extensions.Logging;
using System.Text.Json.Serialization;
using System.Text.Json;
using System.Text;

public class RestSvc(HttpClient httpClient, ILogger<RestSvc> log)
{
    // Define a method for sending asynchronous HTTP requests
    public async Task<T> SendAsync<T>(HttpMethod httpMethod, string url,
     object bodyObj = null, string contentType = "application/json",
     Dictionary<string, string> headers = null, TimeSpan? timeout = null,
     byte retry = 1, short delay = 5)
    {
        //Create an HttpRequestMessage with the specified HTTP method and URL
        var httpRequestMessage = new HttpRequestMessage(httpMethod, url);

        // Add custom headers to the HttpRequestMessage if provided
        if (headers != null)
        {
            foreach (var header in headers)
                httpRequestMessage.Headers.TryAddWithoutValidation(
                                    header.Key, header.Value);
        }

        // Serialize the request body object to JSON and set it as the
        // content of the HttpRequestMessage
        if (bodyObj != null)
        {
          httpRequestMessage.Content = new StringContent(
          JsonSerializer.Serialize(bodyObj), Encoding.UTF8,"application/json");

            // Set the content type header if provided
            if (!string.IsNullOrEmpty(contentType))
            {
                httpRequestMessage.Content.Headers.ContentType = new
                    System.Net.Http.Headers.MediaTypeHeaderValue(contentType);
            }
        }
```

```csharp
// Set the timeout for the HttpClient if provided
if (timeout != null)
{
    httpClient.Timeout = timeout.Value;
}

// Retry sending the request for the specified number of times
for (int i = 1; i <= retry; i++)
{
    string str = string.Empty;

    try
    {
        // Send the HttpRequestMessage and get the response
        HttpResponseMessage res = await
                    httpClient.SendAsync(httpRequestMessage);

        // Read the response content as a string
        str = await res.Content.ReadAsStringAsync();

        // Deserialize the response content to the specified generic
        // type and return it
        return Deserialize<T>(str);
    }
    catch (Exception e)
    {
        // Log any exceptions that occur during the request
        log.LogError(e, $"{httpMethod} - {url}, body: {str}");
    }

    // Delay before retrying the request
    await Task.Delay(delay * 1000);
}

// If all retries fail, return the default value of the generic type
return default(T);
}

// Deserialize the JSON string to the specified generic type
```

```csharp
    private T Deserialize<T>(this string str)
    {
        // Configure the JSON deserialization options
        JsonSerializerOptions deserializeOptions = new()
        {
            PropertyNameCaseInsensitive = true,
            Converters = { new JsonStringEnumConverter() }
        };

        // Deserialize the JSON string to the specified generic type and
        // return it
        return JsonSerializer.Deserialize<T>(str, deserializeOptions);
    }
}
```

```csharp
public class FullName
{
    public string FirstName { get; set; }
    public string LastName { get; set; }
}

public class MyService(RestSvc rest)
{
    public async Task SendJson()
    {
        string url = "https://api.example.com";
        var body = new { Id = 5 };
        var response = await rest.SendAsync<FullName>(HttpMethod.Post, url, body);
    }
}
```

HttpRequestMessage

HttpRequestMessage class provides several properties and methods to work with HTTP requests.

Method: Gets or sets the HTTP method used by the request (e.g., GET, POST, PUT, DELETE).

RequestUri: Gets or sets the URI of the requested resource.

Content: Gets or sets the HTTP request content as an HttpContent object.

Headers: Gets the collection of HTTP headers associated with the request.

Version: Gets or sets the HTTP version used by the request.

Properties: Gets a collection of properties for the HTTP request.

```csharp
var request = new HttpRequestMessage(HttpMethod.Get, "https://api.site.com");

// Setting headers
request.Headers.Add("User-Agent", "MyUserAgent");
request.Headers.Accept.Add(new MediaTypeWithQualityHeaderValue("application/json"));

// Setting content for POST requests
request.Content = new StringContent("Request Content", Encoding.UTF8,
                                    "application/json");

// Accessing properties
request.Properties["MyCustomProperty"] = "CustomValue";
```

HttpResponseMessage

HttpResponseMessage is a class that represents an HTTP response message received from a web server after sending an HTTP request. It contains information such as the status code, headers, and the response body. Here are some of the commonly used properties and methods of the HttpResponseMessage class:

Properties

Content: Gets or sets the HTTP response content as an HttpContent object.

Headers: Gets the collection of HTTP headers associated with the response.

IsSuccessStatusCode: Gets a value that indicates whether the HTTP response was successful (status code in the 2xx range).

ReasonPhrase: Gets the reason phrase that is contained in the HTTP response.

RequestMessage: Gets or sets the request message that was sent to the server.

StatusCode: Gets the HTTP status code returned by the server.

Methods

Dispose(): Releases the unmanaged resources used by the HttpResponseMessage class.

EnsureSuccessStatusCode(): Throws an exception if the HTTP status code of the response is not a success code (i.e., not in the 2xx range).

Content.ReadAsStringAsync(): Asynchronously reads the HTTP response content as a string.

Content.ReadAsStreamAsync(): Asynchronously reads the HTTP response content as a stream.

```csharp
// Create an instance of HttpClient
using HttpClient client = new();

HttpRequestMessage request = new(HttpMethod.Get, "https://api.site.com");

try
{
    // Send the request asynchronously
    HttpResponseMessage response = await client.SendAsync(request);

    // Example of HttpResponseMessage properties
    Console.WriteLine($"IsSuccessStatusCode: {response.IsSuccessStatusCode}");
    Console.WriteLine($"StatusCode: {response.StatusCode}");
    Console.WriteLine($"ReasonPhrase: {response.ReasonPhrase}");
    Console.WriteLine($"RequestMessage: {response.RequestMessage}");

    if (response.IsSuccessStatusCode)
    {
        // Reading response content as string
        string responseBody = await response.Content.ReadAsStringAsync();
        Console.WriteLine("Response content: " + responseBody);
    }
    else
```

```csharp
    {
        // Ensure success status code
        response.EnsureSuccessStatusCode();
    }
}
catch (HttpRequestException ex)
{
    Console.WriteLine("HTTP request error: " + ex.Message);
}
catch (Exception ex)
{
    Console.WriteLine("Error: " + ex.Message);
}
```

IHttpClientFactory

IHttpClientFactory is an interface for creating and managing instances of HttpClient. It is used to centralize and configure the creation of HttpClient instances in a way that promotes reuse and better resource management, especially in scenarios like making multiple HTTP requests to different endpoints within an application.

Basic usage

```
builder.Services.AddHttpClient();
```

```
public class MyService(IHttpClientFactory httpClientFactory)
{
    public void Func()
    {
        HttpClient httpClient = httpClientFactory.CreateClient();
    }
}
```

By default, when you call CreateClient() on an instance of HttpClientFactory, it will either return a new instance of HttpClient or a previously created instance from an internal pool, depending on the configuration. This behavior is controlled by the lifetime management options provided during the registration of the HttpClient with the HttpClientFactory.

Named clients

By using named HttpClient instances, you can have different configurations for different API endpoints or services within your application. This approach allows you to centralize configuration and manage HttpClient instances more efficiently using HttpClientFactory.

Each named HttpClient instance is configured with a different base address and default authorization header.

```
builder.Services.AddHttpClient("GitHub", httpClient =>
{
    httpClient.BaseAddress = new Uri("https://api.github.com");
    httpClient.DefaultRequestHeaders.Add(HeaderNames.Authorization, "1234");
});
```

```csharp
builder.Services.AddHttpClient("Youtube", httpClient =>
{
    httpClient.BaseAddress = new Uri("https://api.youtube.com");
    httpClient.DefaultRequestHeaders.Add(HeaderNames.Authorization, "4321");
});
```

```csharp
public class MyService(IHttpClientFactory httpClientFactory)
{
    public void Func()
    {
        HttpClient gitHubHttpClient = httpClientFactory.CreateClient("GitHub");
        HttpClient youtubeHttpClient = httpClientFactory.CreateClient("Youtube");
    }
}
```

Typed clients

The usage of typed HttpClient, where you define a strongly typed client class that consumes HttpClient.

```csharp
public class MyClient(HttpClient httpClient)
{
    public async Task GetDataAsync()
    {
        var response = await httpClient.GetAsync("https://api.site.com");
    }
}
```

```csharp
builder.Services.AddHttpClient<MyClient>();
```

```csharp
public class MyService(MyClient myClient)
{
    public void Func()
    {
        var response = myClient.GetDataAsync();
    }
}
```

Overall, this pattern allows you to abstract away the HttpClient-related logic into a separate client class (MyClient), making your code cleaner, more maintainable, and easier to test. It also ensures that HttpClient instances are managed efficiently by the HttpClientFactory.

Generated Clients

Generated clients can be created using third-party libraries like Refit or NSwag. These libraries can generate strongly typed HTTP clients based on API contracts or OpenAPI/Swagger specifications

gRPC

gRPC is an open-source remote procedure call (RPC) system initially developed by Google. It uses HTTP/2 for transport, Protocol Buffers as the interface description language, and provides features such as authentication, load balancing, and more. gRPC allows client and server applications to communicate transparently, enabling efficient and fast communication between distributed systems.

gRPC vs HTTP

gRPC and HTTP are two different communication protocols, each with its own strengths and weaknesses. The choice between gRPC and HTTP depends on various factors such as performance requirements, communication patterns, language interoperability, and ecosystem support. Here's a comparison to help you understand why you might choose gRPC over HTTP:

Performance: gRPC typically offers better performance compared to traditional HTTP APIs. It achieves this by using HTTP/2 as the underlying transport protocol, which allows for multiplexing multiple RPC calls over a single connection, reducing latency and overhead. gRPC also supports binary serialization using Protocol Buffers, which can be more efficient than text-based formats like JSON used in HTTP APIs.

Strongly Typed Contracts: gRPC uses Protocol Buffers for defining service contracts (.proto files). Protocol Buffers provide a strongly typed interface definition language, enabling automatic generation of client and server code in multiple languages. This can help reduce errors and make development more productive, especially in large-scale projects with multiple teams.

Bidirectional Streaming: gRPC supports bidirectional streaming, where both the client and server can send a stream of messages asynchronously. This is useful for scenarios such as real-time communication, telemetry, or video streaming, where continuous data exchange is required.

However, it's important to note that gRPC might not be the best choice for every scenario. Here are some reasons you might choose traditional HTTP APIs over gRPC:

Simplicity: HTTP APIs are simpler to understand and work with, especially for developers unfamiliar with Protocol Buffers or binary serialization. They are also well-suited for human-readable data formats like JSON, which are easier to debug and troubleshoot.

Existing Infrastructure: If you already have a large codebase or infrastructure built around HTTP APIs, migrating to gRPC might require significant effort and may not be justified unless you have specific performance or scalability requirements that cannot be met with HTTP.

Client Compatibility: Some clients, particularly web browsers and mobile devices, may have limited support for gRPC compared to traditional HTTP APIs. In such cases, using HTTP APIs may be more practical for reaching a wider audience.

In summary, while gRPC offers several advantages over traditional HTTP APIs in terms of performance, type safety, and language interoperability, the choice between gRPC and HTTP depends on your specific requirements, existing infrastructure, and the trade-offs you are willing to make.

Create gRPC Server

gRPC ASP.NET Core gRPC Service

A project template for creating a gRPC service using ASP.NET

C#   Linux   macOS   Windows   Cloud   Service

Define service contract and implement gRPC service

Define your service and message types using Protocol Buffers. Protocol Buffers define the structure of your messages and services in a language-neutral way.

The code below defines a service named Users with an RPC method GetUserNames that takes a UserIds message (containing an array of IDs) and returns a UserNames message (containing an array of UserInfo objects with first names and last names).

Create users.proto file inside Protos folder.

users.proto

```protobuf
// Specify that this file uses Protocol Buffers version 3 syntax
syntax = "proto3";


// Specify the C# namespace for the generated code
option csharp_namespace = "GrpcServices";


// Define the package name for the Protocol Buffers definitions in this file
package users;


// Define the gRPC service named Users
service Users {
  // Define an RPC method named GetUserNames
  rpc GetUserNames(UserIds) returns (UserNames);
}


// Define a message type to hold a list of user IDs
message UserIds {
  // Define a field to hold the list of user IDs
  repeated int32 ids = 1;
}


// Define a message type to hold a list of user names
message UserNames {
  // Define a field to hold the list of user information
  repeated UserInfo users = 1;
}


// Define a message type to represent information about a user
message UserInfo {
  // Define a field to hold the user's first name
  string first_name = 1;
  // Define a field to hold the user's last name
  string last_name = 2;
}
```

Create the logic of the service:

GrpcUsersService.cs

GrpcUsersService inherits from Users.UsersBase. Users.UsersBase is a generated base class that contains the service definition from the Protocol Buffers file.

```csharp
public class GrpcUsersService : Users.UsersBase
{
    //Implementation of the gRPC method defined in the Protocol Buffers file.
    public override Task<UserNames> GetUserNames(UserIds request,
                                ServerCallContext context)
    {
        var users = new List<UserInfo>();

        foreach (var id in request.Ids)
        {
            // Example: Fetch user information from a data source
            var userInfo = FetchUserInfoFromDatabase(id);

            if (userInfo != null)
            {
                users.Add(userInfo);
            }
        }
        return Task.FromResult(new UserNames { Users = { users } });
    }


    // Example method to fetch user information from a database.
    private UserInfo FetchUserInfoFromDatabase(int id)
    {
        // For simplicity, we'll just return some hardcoded values.
        return new UserInfo
        {
            FirstName = "Eldar",
            LastName = "Cohen"
        };
    }
}
```

Program.cs

```
builder.Services.AddGrpc();

app.MapGrpcService<GrpcUsersService>();
```

Consume gRPC service

Create new console project.

Copy the users.proto file to the project.

Add to the .csproj file this code:

```
<ItemGroup>
  <Protobuf Include="Protos\users.proto" GrpcServices="Client" />
</ItemGroup>
```

Use the client:

```csharp
// Create a gRPC channel to communicate with the server
var channel = GrpcChannel.ForAddress("http://localhost:5222");


// Create a gRPC client for the Users service using the created channel
var client = new Users.UsersClient(channel);


// Create an instance of UserIds message to hold user IDs
var userIds = new UserIds();


// Add user IDs to the UserIds message
userIds.Ids.Add(1);
userIds.Ids.Add(2);


// Call the GetUserNames method of the gRPC
var userNames = client.GetUserNames(userIds);


foreach (var userInfo in userNames.Users)
{
    Console.WriteLine($"User: {userInfo.FirstName} {userInfo.LastName}");
}


// Shutdown the gRPC channel
channel.ShutdownAsync().Wait();
```

HTTPS

ASP.NET supports HTTPS (HTTP over SSL/TLS) for secure communication between clients (such as web browsers) and web servers. Enabling HTTPS ensures that data transmitted between the client and the server is encrypted and secure, protecting sensitive information from interception or tampering.

UseHsts

UseHsts() is a middleware to add HTTP Strict Transport Security (HSTS) policy to the HTTP response headers.

HTTP Strict Transport Security (HSTS) is a security feature that informs the browser that it should only interact with the server over secure HTTPS connections. It helps protect against downgrade attacks and cookie hijacking. Once the browser has received the HSTS header from the server, it will only access the website over HTTPS for the specified duration, even if the user attempts to access it via HTTP.

Program.cs

```
app.UseHsts();
```

UseHttpsRedirection

UseHttpsRedirection() is a middleware used to configure automatic redirection from HTTP to HTTPS. When this middleware is enabled, any HTTP requests received by the application are automatically redirected to their HTTPS counterparts.

Program.cs

```
app.UseHttpsRedirection()
```

Swagger

Swagger is a framework for designing, building, documenting, and consuming RESTful APIs. It allows to define the structure of an APIs using a standard format called OpenAPI Specification (formerly known as Swagger Specification). ASP.NET developers can use Swagger to automatically generate interactive API documentation.

You can then use the Swagger UI interface to interact with the API, such as testing different endpoints, providing request parameters, and viewing responses. This helps in understanding how your API works and how clients can interact with it.

To integrate Swagger with ASP.NET, you can use various libraries and tools such as Swashbuckle. Swashbuckle is a popular package for ASP.NET Web API projects that automatically generates Swagger documentation based on your API controllers, routes, and models.

Install: Swashbuckle.AspNetCore

Swashbuckle.AspNetCore by Swashbuckle.AspNetCore,
Swagger tools for documenting APIs built on ASP.NET Core

Program.cs

```
//Adds Swagger services to the service collection

builder.Services.AddSwaggerGen();


//adds middleware to your request pipeline that enables serving the //generated Swagger JSON
document. This allows other tools or clients to //access the raw API documentation.
app.UseSwagger();


//adds middleware to your request pipeline that serves the Swagger UI. This //is a web interface
that allows users to explore and interact with the API //documentation in a more user-friendly way.
app.UseSwaggerUI();
```

Let's create User crud endpoints:

```
public class User
{
    public int UserId { get; set; }
    public string FirstName { get; set; }
    public string LastName { get; set; }
}
```

212

```csharp
[Route("api/[controller]")]
[ApiController]
public class UserController : ControllerBase
{
    [HttpGet] public User Get(int id){ return new User(); }

    [HttpPost] public void Post([FromBody] User user){ }

    [HttpPut] public void Put([FromBody] User user) { }

    [HttpDelete] public void Delete(int id) { }
}
```

Let's, run the server in url: https://localhost:7232/swagger

WebApplication3 1.0 OAS3

https://localhost:7232/swagger/v1/swagger.json

User ⌃

| GET | /api/User | ⌄ |

| POST | /api/User | ⌄ |

| PUT | /api/User | ⌄ |

| DELETE | /api/User | ⌄ |

Schemas ⌃

```
User ⌄ {
    userId              integer($int32)
    firstName           string
                        nullable: true
    lastName            string
                        nullable: true
}
```

Now you to easily test your APIs.

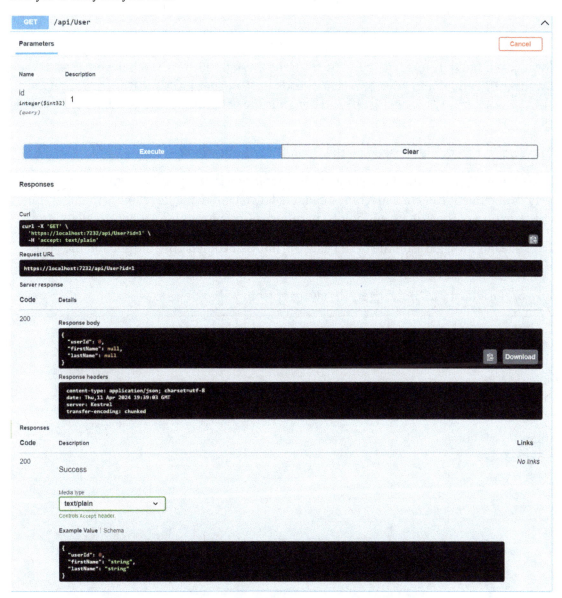

When you open the GET action in Swagger UI and execute it, you will see a response.

Swagger UI will show you the details of the request parameters for the GET action.

Request URL: Swagger UI will display the URL that will be called when you execute the request.

Response: After executing the request, Swagger UI will display the response received from the server in JSON format.

Response Status: Swagger UI will also show the HTTP status code returned by the server. For a successful request, it should be 200 OK.

swagger.json

Swagger UI build its interface directly from the Swagger JSON file. When you access the Swagger UI endpoint in your browser it reads the Swagger JSON file from the provided URL (/swagger/v1/swagger.json) and dynamically generates the user interface based on the information in that JSON file.

The Swagger JSON file is based on the OpenAPI Specification.

The OpenAPI Specification is a standard format for describing RESTful APIs. It provides a way to document APIs in a machine-readable format, allowing developers to understand the structure of the API, its endpoints, parameters, responses, and other details.

Let's see our swagger.json file of the user api above. I copied only the get and the post methods.

https://localhost:7232/swagger/v1/swagger.json

```json
{
  "openapi": "3.0.1",
  "info": {
    "title": "WebApplication3",
    "version": "1.0"
  },
  "paths": {
    "/api/User": {
      "get": {
        "tags": [
          "User"
        ],
        "parameters": [
          {
            "name": "id",
            "in": "query",
            "schema": {
              "type": "integer",
              "format": "int32"
            }
          }
        ],
        "responses": {
          "200": {
            "description": "Success",
            "content": {
              "text/plain": {
```

```json
          "schema": {
            "$ref": "#/components/schemas/User"
          }
        },
        "application/json": {
          "schema": {
            "$ref": "#/components/schemas/User"
          }
        },
        "text/json": {
          "schema": {
            "$ref": "#/components/schemas/User"
          }
        }
      }
    }
  }
},
"post": {
  "tags": [
    "User"
  ],
  "requestBody": {
    "content": {
      "application/json": {
        "schema": {
          "$ref": "#/components/schemas/User"
        }
      },
      "text/json": {
        "schema": {
          "$ref": "#/components/schemas/User"
        }
      },
      "application/*+json": {
        "schema": {
          "$ref": "#/components/schemas/User"
        }
      }
    }
  },
  "responses": {
    "200": {
      "description": "Success"
    }
```

```json
        }
       }
      }
    },
    "components": {
     "schemas": {
      "User": {
       "type": "object",
       "properties": {
        "userId": {
         "type": "integer",
         "format": "int32"
        },
        "firstName": {
         "type": "string",
         "nullable": true
        },
        "lastName": {
         "type": "string",
         "nullable": true
        }
       },
       "additionalProperties": false
      }
     }
    }
}
```

Deploy ASP.NET Application

Here's a guide on how to deploy an ASP.NET application on a Windows.

VPS

1. Buy vps on https://contabo.com or other vps service.

   Virtual Private Servers (VPS) are a popular choice for hosting websites, and other online services. VPS act as a dedicated server with its own operating system.

2. Configure the machine and.

Windows Server

3. install windows server on the machine.

   Windows Server is a operating systems designed by Microsoft for server deployments. It provides a wide range of features and capabilities tailored for various server roles, including file and print services, web hosting, application hosting, database management, virtualization, networking, and more. Windows Server is available in several editions.

Core Runtime, Hosting Bundle

4. Download and install on you server ASP.NET Core Runtime, Hosting Bundle

   https://dotnet.microsoft.com/en-us/download

   The ASP.NET Core Runtime is a set of libraries and components required to run ASP.NET applications. It includes the .NET runtime, ASP.NET libraries, and other dependencies necessary for hosting and executing ASP.NET web applications. The runtime provides the necessary infrastructure to handle HTTP requests, process application logic, and serve responses.

   The ASP.NET Hosting Bundle is a package that includes both the ASP.NET Core Runtime and the .NET Core Runtime optimized for hosting ASP.NET Core applications on a server. It also includes the ASP.NET Core Module for IIS (Internet Information Services) integration, which allows you to host ASP.NET Core applications on Windows servers running IIS.

5. Install IIS on your server.

Internet Information Services (IIS) is a web server software developed by Microsoft for hosting websites, web applications, and services on Windows servers. It provides a robust and scalable platform for serving HTTP, HTTPS, FTP, SMTP, and other web protocols. Open Server Manager - > Add Roles and Features:

Role-based or feature-based installation and click Next:

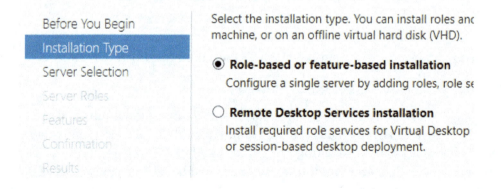

Select the appropriate server and click Next:

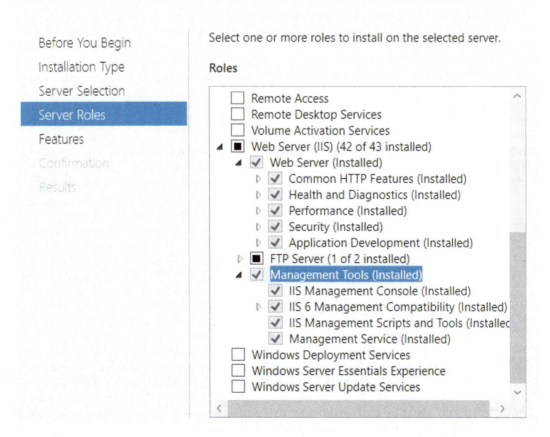

Scroll down and check the box Web Server (IIS).

You can optionally add additional features if required.

Review the selections you've made, and then click Install to begin the installation process.

Select server roles

6. Buy domain for your site, use https://porkbun.com or other domain service you want. Let say you bought the domain site.com, you need to set the domain in porkbun admin panel to direct to your server ip address that you can see in your vps admin control panel.

7. Publish your asp.net app. Right click on the project and click publish:

Choose folder, click next, choose folder path, click finish:

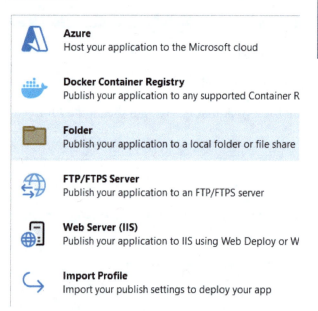

Make sure your configuration is set to release and click publish:

Enter the folder path you selected previously and copy the files generated to your vps to the folder c:\sites\myapp

Enter IIS in your vps.

Right click on sites folder.

Click on Add Website:

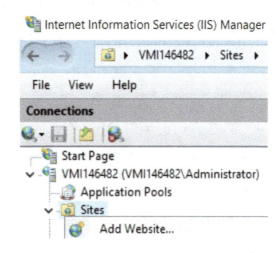

Fill any site name you want.

Fill the path of your app files.

Fill the domain you bought.

Press ok.

Now you can enter your domain site.com the site should work.

When you update the DNS (Domain Name System) for a domain, such as changing the IP address associated with the domain, it can take some time for the changes to propagate across the internet. This delay is known as DNS propagation.

So, you maybe you'll need to wait until the domain will work.

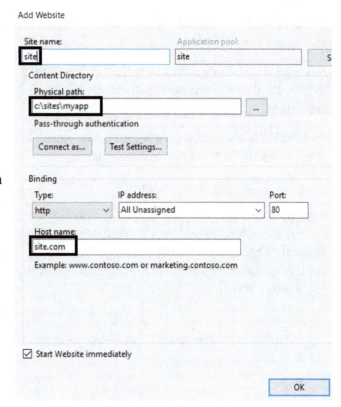

Host file

If you want to run you asp.net app in your development pc with the domain instead localhost:port, you can use the windows host file.

The hosts file is a plain text file used by operating systems like Windows, macOS, and Linux to map hostnames to IP addresses before querying a DNS (Domain Name System) server. It is typically located in the following directories:

Windows: C:\Windows\System32\drivers\etc\

macOS: /private/etc/

Linux: /etc/

Each line in the hosts file contains an IP address followed by one or more hostnames separated by spaces or tabs. 127.0.0.1 site.com

Adding 127.0.0.1 site.com to the hosts file will direct requests for the domain "site.com" to your local machine, specifically to the loopback address (127.0.0.1), bypassing DNS resolution.

127.0.0.1: This is the loopback address of your local machine. It always refers back to the same machine that you are currently using.

site.com: This is the domain name you want to map to the loopback address.

By adding this entry to your hosts file, any requests made to "site.com" will be redirected to your local machine, allowing you to test your website or web application locally without needing a public DNS entry or internet access. Remember to remove or comment out this entry when you no longer need it, especially if "site.com" is a real domain that you need to access on the internet.

Export/Import IIS sites

To copy IIS sites from one server to another, or for backup purposes, you can follow these steps.

Open Command Prompt as an Administrator.

Export:

cd C:\Windows\System32\inetsrv

appcmd list site /config /xml > C:\iis-sites.xml

appcmd list apppool /config /xml > C:\iis-app-pools.xml

Import:

cd %windir%\system32\inetsrv

appcmd add site /in < C:\iis-sites.xml

appcmd add apppool /in < C:\iis-app-pools.xml

Ensure you manually copy the website content (files and folders) from the source server to the destination server.

Host ASP.NET as a Windows Service

Hosting ASP.NET applications as Windows services instead of using IIS (Internet Information Services) has its own set of use cases and advantages:

Control: Hosting ASP.NET applications as Windows services gives you more control over the hosting environment. You have the flexibility to manage the application lifecycle, including starting, stopping, and monitoring the service, without relying on IIS.

No dependency on IIS: By hosting as a Windows service, you eliminate the dependency on IIS. This can be beneficial in scenarios where you want to avoid potential conflicts with other applications or configurations on the IIS server.

Portability: Windows services can be deployed on any Windows machine without requiring IIS to be installed. This can be useful for scenarios where you need to deploy the application on machines where IIS might not be available or appropriate.

Performance: In some cases, hosting ASP.NET applications as Windows services can provide better performance compared to running them under IIS. This is because Windows services have lower overhead and fewer layers of abstraction compared to IIS.

Isolation: Running the application as a Windows service provides a level of isolation from other applications running on the same machine. This can be important for security and stability reasons, especially in shared hosting environments.

However, it's essential to consider that hosting ASP.NET applications as Windows services also has its limitations and trade-offs. For example, managing routing, load balancing, and other web server functionalities typically provided by IIS would need to be handled separately if you choose to host as a Windows service. Additionally, you may miss out on some of the built-in features and optimizations that IIS offers for hosting ASP.NET applications.

Install package: Microsoft.Extensions.Hosting.WindowsServices

 Microsoft.Extensions.Hosting.WindowsServices
.NET hosting infrastructure for Windows Services.

Program.cs

```
builder.Services.AddWindowsService();
```

Server signature

In ASP.NET, it's a good practice to turn off the server signature for security reasons. The server signature is an HTTP response header that provides information about the server software, such as the server name and version. Exposing this information can make it easier for attackers to identify vulnerabilities specific to the server software version you are using.

Here's how you can turn off the server signature in different environments:

IIS (Internet Information Services)

If you are hosting your ASP.NET application on IIS, you can turn off the server signature by modifying the web.config file and using the httpProtocol section. Here's how you can do it:

Edit the web.config File:

Add the following configuration to the <system.webServer> section of your web.config file:

```xml
<?xml version="1.0" encoding="utf-8"?>
<configuration>
    <system.webServer>
        <httpProtocol>
            <customHeaders>
                <remove name="X-Powered-By" />
                <remove name="Server" />
            </customHeaders>
        </httpProtocol>
    </system.webServer>
</configuration>
```

Middleware

For an ASP.NET Core application, you can turn off the server signature by configuring the web server and modifying the response headers within your application with a custom middleware:

```csharp
public class RemoveServerHeaderMiddleware
{
    private readonly RequestDelegate _next;

    public RemoveServerHeaderMiddleware(RequestDelegate next)
    {
        _next = next;
    }

    public async Task Invoke(HttpContext context)
    {
        context.Response.OnStarting(() =>
        {
            context.Response.Headers.Remove("Server");
            context.Response.Headers.Remove("X-Powered-By");
            return Task.CompletedTask;
        });

        await _next(context);
    }
}
```

Performance Optimization

To make your server go faster, here are some strategies you can consider:

Optimize Code and Queries

Code Efficiency: Review your code for any inefficient loops, recursive functions, or unnecessary computations. Refactor code for better performance.

Query Optimization: Analyze and optimize database queries to reduce execution time. Avoid unnecessary joins and ensure indexes are correctly used. Use pagination to prevent large datasets from overwhelming the server. If you need to query multiple items, combine them into a single query when possible.

API Calls: Enable Gzip or Brotli compression to reduce response sizes. Where possible, combine multiple operations into a single API endpoint to reduce the number of requests.

Asynchronous Processing

Using asynchronous operations prevents blocking the main thread during operations. When dealing with databases, file operations, or APIs, asynchronous methods can significantly enhance performance and responsiveness, particularly in scenarios where these operations might be slow or blocking. Asynchronous operations enable the application to continue processing other tasks while waiting for these operations to complete.

Avoid async/await where it's not needed to reduce context-switching overhead.

Message Queues

Using message queues like RabbitMQ and Amazon SQS etc, can significantly improve asynchronous processing by introducing decoupling, scalability, and fault tolerance in distributed systems.

How It Works?

- Add request to a message queue.

- A worker service retrieves the request from the queue and processes it. Processing happens in the background, workers operate independently, enabling parallel execution, load balancing, and fault tolerance.

- Once processed, the worker acknowledges the completion, and the message is removed

Caching

Data Caching: Implement caching mechanisms to store frequently accessed data in memory, reducing the need for repeated database queries and apis calls.

HTTP Caching: Use HTTP caching headers to reduce the load on your server by allowing browsers to cache static content.

Minify and Bundling

Minifying and bundling CSS and JavaScript files to improve the performance of web applications by reducing the amount of data transferred and the number of HTTP requests.

High-Performance Memory Management

Use Span<T> and Memory<T> for high-performance memory management, especially in I/O operations,

Span<T> is a stack-only type that represents a contiguous region of memory. It's designed for high-performance, temporary operations and avoids heap allocations.

Memory<T> is similar to Span<T> but is heap-allocated and can be used across asynchronous and non-stack scenarios. It represents a contiguous region of memory that can be used for longer-term operations.

Load Balancing

Use a load balancer to distribute traffic across multiple servers. This helps manage higher traffic loads and improves reliability.

Server Instances

Add more servers to handle increased traffic.

CDN

Content Delivery Network (CDN): Serve static content (like images, CSS, and JavaScript files) via a CDN. This reduces the load on your server and speeds up content delivery to users globally.

Profiling and Monitoring

Profiling: Use profiling tools to identify and optimize slow parts of your application.

Monitoring: Set up monitoring to track performance metrics (like response times, CPU usage, memory usage) and detect issues early.

Hardware

Adding more hardware resources like CPU, memory, and SSD can improve the performance

Use JWT instead of Sessions

Since JWTs contain all the necessary information within the token itself, you don't need to store session data on the server. This reduces the server's memory footprint and eliminates the need to synchronize session data across multiple servers.

No Sticky Sessions: Sticky sessions (or session affinity) are used to ensure that a user's requests are always routed to the same server. With JWTs, this isn't necessary because any server can validate the token. This makes load balancing and horizontal scaling easier. Adding more servers to handle increased traffic becomes simpler. You can distribute the load without worrying about session consistency across servers.